HAUNTED

HAUNTED

STORIES OF SPIRITS, SCOUNDRELS, LEGENDS, LORE, AND GHOSTS IN THE RIALTO THEATER AND DOWNTOWN EL DORADO, ARKANSAS

RICHARD MASON

BWM BOOKS PTY LTD
CANBERRA

CONTENTS

FOREWORD

THIS book is a work of fiction. The representation of rumors, whispers, and folklore in this novel—which seems to be a factual accounting of an event—is the author's attempt to give readers some glimmer of El Dorado's history, and not to accurately depict a factual representation of what happened there.

I have written this book in a manner that I hope will give the readers a better understanding of the tragic events and paranormal occurrences recorded in and around the Rialto Theater in downtown El Dorado, Arkansas. To do this, I have used historical dialogue to convey the spirit of the times. Without this, the book would only be a simple accounting of events, and a shallow summation of what actually happened.

I believe that understanding the setting and history of this little village is necessary to comprehend the magnitude of the tragic events and paranormal occurrences that have been documented. Fictional dialogue will help readers better understand the enormity of these soul-wrenching events that altered the character of the community.

In order to adequately depict the mass of humanity that flooded El Dorado during the early 1920s oil boom and created so many chaotic situations, I have inserted several pages of material from my historical novel, *The Queen of Hamburger Row*. Without an understanding of something as earthshaking as the oil boom of the 1920s and the resulting mayhem and violence, it would be difficult to fully comprehend this bucolic place we now call downtown El Dorado.

How could the seemingly quiet town we see today have been a witness to so many horrific events and paranormal occurrences?

In order to document the material presented in this book, I have conducted personal interviews and used recorded historical remembrances from the Arkansas Museum of Natural Resources. My own interviews and the museum interviews are from men and women who lived through the 1920s oil boom. In a number of these interviews, the people telling their stories repeated conversations heard from grandmothers and great-grandmothers or grandfathers. I used this second-hand information to complete the early historical record of the community.

These interviews—combined with the current tales of paranormal sighting, smells, and noises in the theater or in the area near the theater—have fleshed out the book.

In order to record a complete history of this little downtown El Dorado gem, the Rialto Theatre, I have pieced together and interpreted many of the rumors. Some of the events described are based on the flimsiest of evidence, but they have been included to give completeness to the investigation, and to contribute to the overall goal of the book, which is to record as much as I can of the paranormal and tragic events of the past.

After considering the connection between the huge number of violent, unsolved murders, gunfights, and other horrific events that took place in El Dorado's history, I have concluded that they are directly related to the paranormal experiences in the community. In other words, I believe many of the spirits that haunt downtown El Dorado do so because they are directly related to tragic past events, including unsolved murders.

So, as you read this collection of wild tales, understand that definitive evidence of an event or a paranormal occurrence may be rather slim—and, yes, I have taken some of the rumors and extrapolated them into what seems to be actual happenings. But if you consider the overall scope of this investigation, I believe you will recognize a thread of historic violence and paranormal occurrences running through this town, which gives El Dorado the unwanted distinction of having one of the most violent histories imaginable.

I am convinced that this town's past is directly related to its hundreds of paranormal occurrences, which has earned this little village the title as one of the most haunted towns in America, along with being a town with an unbelievable notorious history. And the two are directly related.

1

RIALTO GHOSTS

ADA Williams, a longtime theater manager, told me a number of strange stories concerning paranormal activities in the Rialto Theater. Her comments are typical of many that have been recounted, especially her observations about sightings in and around the women's rest room.

To quote Ada Williams:

"Practically every projectionist has had an experience in the upstairs booth and around the lady's rest room: the report about smelling women's perfume, feeling a brush of air as if someone walked by, doors opening and closing, the feeling that someone was in the room, and that they were not alone. Sometimes they would report a definite odor of cigar smoke, even to the point of seeing a blue haze. Of course, almost all of them report seeing the white mist that suddenly appears and floats around for a few minutes, and then disappears as quickly as it appeared.

"Another experience I can remember occurred late one night when two workers were in the downstairs booth during the off hours, with all the doors locked. Both distinctly heard someone climbing the circular stairs. They checked upstairs and found no one. They did mention they saw the door swing shut in the lady's rest room just as they topped the stairs, but they were afraid to check to see if anyone was in there. Of course, the theater doors were locked so no one could have come in while they were in the projection booth.

"There have been numerous other sighting in and around the lady's rest room, and I guess of all the places in the theater, more strange things have been reported from that area than anywhere in the theater.

"I remember one very well: A lady in period dress—it evidently was a-turn-of-the- century dress—was wearing a long, flowing, veiled hat. (Pate mentioned a very similar spirit here.) She entered the rest room, then disappeared. Different types of shoes including button-ups have been seen in stalls with no one there."

(Author's note: The description of a woman wearing a vintage dress in the lady's rest room has been reported numerous times. I've concluded that it's the spirit of a vaudeville actress in costume.)

Williams continued to describe the numerous sightings and sounds that she and her staff had experienced.

"An elderly woman was seen entering the men's room, then disappeared—Heavy boots/shoes/footsteps were heard walking across the tile in the concession area several times.

"I was in the projection booth in the main auditorium with a projectionist one evening, and we were the only ones in the theater. We locked ourselves in the booth and were doing some maintenance on the equipment when I distinctly heard someone climb the winding staircase. I looked at my projectionist and asked him, 'Did you hear that?' He said 'Yes ma'am, I did.'

"'What did you hear?' I said. 'I heard someone climb the staircase.' So he took my pistol and went all over the upstairs and never saw anyone. But I definitely heard footsteps. They faded away like they were climbing stairs, and I know for a fact there was no one in the theater. We had locked ourselves in." (Williams recounted this to a newspaper interviewer a few years back.)

The stories about mysterious sounds and smells have been almost continuous since the early days of the theater. Gabriel, a young employee during the 1990s had multiple encounters with a ghost during his employment at the theater. The most vivid one occurred late one evening when he saw something in the main auditorium—something that made him nearly incoherent.

Ada Williams, who was with Gabriel, described it this way:

"We were in the main auditorium one night—it was around 10 p.m..—and we were walking down the aisle. He was on the right-hand side, and about a third of the way down. He started looking up and started rotating, just turning as if he were watching something in the ceiling. I kept asking him what was going on, and he just got hysterical and started screaming at me, 'Don't you see it? Don't you see it?' I never saw anything, and when he finally got coherent, he said it was like a cloud of white mist and that it floated across the ceiling and went into the balcony—right through the balcony wall. He definitely saw something, and he smelled the perfume."

(Author's note: numerous individuals have noted this cloud of mist. Another observation is that when paranormal experiences occur, the spirit frequently will make itself known to only one person, even though several individuals may be in the room. The smell of perfume and the smell of a cigar indicates to me that the spirit present is either female or male.)

This incident, as well as numerous others, has caused the management and workers of the theater to suspect that at least one of the spirit-ghosts is a woman. Evidently, this ghost selectively makes herself known to a person, usually accompanied by the strong smell of perfume. Most of the descriptions are of a white, misty shape—sometimes cloud-like—that floats through the theater, but not always. Occasionally, someone will actually see the outline of a lady, and other times they will hear a female voice and movement on the stairwell.

Williams further commented,

> "As you compare the sightings and the smell of perfume from the theater, one thing stands out: Over the years the number of projectionist and workers, who couldn't have known each other, have told the same story about getting a whiff of women's perfume in the projection booth upstairs.
>
> "It's her perfume you smell. It's like she walks by, and you smell her," said Williams. "A female ghost resides in the Rialto. A previous owner nicknamed her Penelope.
>
> "Once, a young janitor was cleaning the theater after hours. He saw something on the staircase that scared him so badly that he threw his keys at it and ran out of the building. He ran three miles to the manager's house and said, 'Mail me my check and keys—I'm not going back in there again!'"
>
> Ada continued, "Over the years, people who worked in the projection booth have reported smelling a sweet perfume and hearing footsteps climbing the stairs to the projection room. When the person opens the projection room door, though, no one is there. Sometimes people on the floor feel the air become cold and heavy."

(Author's note; Pate mentions this as being an indication of spirits being present.)

(Author's note: Evidently, something eerie and very spirit-like is in the very back of the upstairs balcony area where the old original projection booth is located. Did something terrible happen in or around the projection booth, or in one of the back rows of the theater, as rumors say? Many longtime workers think this area of the theater holds at least one of the mysteries of supernatural occurrences.

There have been many stories about young women and the theater; some of the tales go back to the old theater that was partially torn down to build the new (1929), current theater. A recurring story tells of a young couple, engaged to be married, who attended one of the shows when vaudeville performances were playing in the theater. The man took his date into the Rialto and proposed to her. For months, they planned a large society wedding. However, the troupe featured a beautiful blonde singer, who, according to witnesses, was captivating.

In fact, the young man became completely enamored with the singer's appearance. The show was scheduled for three nights and the young man returned to the theater the next night and was standing at the stage door when the show finished and the cast left to walk the two blocks to the Garrett Hotel, where they were staying. He introduced himself at the stage door, handed her a bouquet of red roses, and asked if he could walk her to the hotel.

He told his friends it was love at first sight, and when the vaudeville troupe left El Dorado a few days later, the actress stayed. The next night he took his bride-to-be back into the theater, and told her he was in love with an actress who had starred in the previous show.

The young woman was broken-hearted and soon the theater employees noticed she was back every night. However, they realized she didn't just go take a seat—she walked up and down the aisles jilted and lonely; soon the young woman pined away and died in the Rialto one Saturday night… from a broken heart.

Those who tell this story believe she still roams the aisles of the Rialto looking for her lost love. And when the old theater was torn down to make room for the new Rialto, strange sounds and smells emanated from the wreckage—only to reappear in the new theater. (Since this story mentions a "live performance" it probably dates back to early years of the 1922 theater when there were live performances.)

Additional Experiences of Paranormal Activity

I have listened to and noted story after story about paranormal sightings in and around the Rialto. If I were asked to name the most haunted spot in the theater, I would not hesitate to say: **the ladies' rest room.**

Wynde Green, a concession worker, listed several paranormal experiences that occurred during her 10 years work at the theater. The following is an account of her experiences.

Incident 1. "Late one afternoon, before the theater opened for the evening movie, I was in the concession area getting everything ready. I tuned my back to get some cups, and I heard loud footsteps coming toward me from the lobby entrance. I turned around to see who was there, but there was nobody in the concession area or in the lobby. I turned back to what I was doing and I heard the footsteps leave from the concession stand toward the exit into the lobby. I looked and there wasn't anyone there, and the lobby entrance doors were locked.

Incident 2. "One night, before I left the building for the night, a co-worker and I heard running up the stairs. We both went to see who it was. When we made it to the top of the stairs, the running sound went into the storage room and we heard the door to the storage room open and close. We checked the storage room and the building, from top to bottom, and didn't see anyone."

Incident 3. "One day, before a movie was about to let out, I went upstairs to check the bathrooms and clean the big mirror in the upstairs lobby beside the ladies' bathroom. A little while later I started smelling the scent of a cigar burning, so I went inside the bathroom and saw a big cloud of smoke as if somebody had just taken a big puff, but no one was around or inside the bathroom." (Note: The Spirit Seekers from Louisiana also recorded the smell of cigar smoke. For many years, the theater manager, known as Mr. Robb, was a fixture in the theater. Psychic Carol Pate describes seeing a man standing on the landing of the stairs that lead to the upstairs lobby. Her description fits Mr. Robb, described by many theatergoers as having a cigar stuck in his mouth while he patrolled the theater.)

Incident 4. "Late one night we had just gotten a film in and another co-worker and I decided to put the movie together after everyone left the building from the last show. Everybody was gone and we locked ourselves in the building. We went upstairs and proceeded to put the movie trailer together, and all of a sudden we started hearing the piano play. When we went around the corner to see what was going on, no one was there." (Note: An old piano sits in the upstairs lobby beside the women's rest room.) No one could have possibly entered or left the building because we had locked all the doors!"

Although Pate's experiences were the most vivid of the paranormal events experienced in the theater, others, including one involving a newspaper reporter and his girlfriend, became a well-documented, paranormal experience in the theater.

★★★

The "Caretaker" Ada Williams, claims to have an idea.

"I call myself the Caretaker of the Rialto because it's historic treasure, and I take care of it," said Williams. "There is supposedly a female ghost here. I named her Penelope because I thought she needed a name, and no one could ever pinpoint this ghost enough to say who she was or why she was here."

Williams said she has had several employees who claimed to have seen Penelope or other apparitions. Many of those employees have also described unusual smells or sounds.Despite the conflicts in some stories, people have witnessed inexplicable things at the Rialto over the years, things that can only be labeled with a word often used tongue-in-cheek: "supernatural."

Williams said in 1996, for instance, that a concession worker went to the ladies' rest room upstairs and "came out saying she wasn't going back up there again." The girl's story was that she had encountered a ghost on the second floor—a ghost that had vanished.

"First of all, we get people in different attire who come in here—tuxedos to long dresses to cut-off jeans. So if somebody's dressed kind of odd, we don't pay much attention because we get all kinds. Well, the girl followed a lady into the bathroom one day; she said the woman had on a long dress, just above the ankles, and some of those old high-top shoes you button, and a hat with a veil over it—really nothing unusual for the Rialto.

"Well, the girl follows her in there, and the ladies' room door squeaks and you know if someone enters or exits that door. So she goes in one stall and the veiled lady goes in the other, and when she gets up and goes around, that stall is empty. And this door that squeaks—and I mean, it's a pronounced squeak—has not budged. The veiled lady just disappeared," Williams said.

She added, "About five years later, another employee told a similar story, this time about seeing a pair of feet in the stall beside her—a pair of feet that suddenly disappeared."

Coincidence?

Williams told yet another story of a young janitor cleaning up after the movies one night in 1993; he saw something on the stairwell, threw the keys to his brand-new pickup up the stairs and ran three miles across town to summon the manager.

"The manager got out of bed, goes and gets the kid and brings him back here, and the boy tells him he was cleaning up when he saw these bright lights up the staircase. He threw his keys at them and ran out the door, and he wouldn't come back in for the life of him. He sat outside while the manager found his keys. He told the manager, "Mail me my check; I won't be back to pick it up." He was very scared to death. And you can verify that story with the manager," Williams stated.

Finally, she commented as we finished the tour, "We have often talked about how much money it would take for someone to stay overnight. No one has volunteered so far so we don't know."

Other stories of paranormal activities come from former employees—sometimes handed down to sons and daughters. Recently, I received an e-mail from a lady with some very interesting comments about the activities in the theater noted by her father, a longtime projectionist there. Following is the e-mail, printed verbatim.

"Mr. Mason, please let me introduce myself, my name is Genie Osborne Williamson, and I live in Prairie Village KS. A longtime friend of mine in El Dorado sent me the Sunday article about the Rialto and the ghosts. My father at the age of 18 came to work as a projectionist at the Rialto in 1930 and was employed there for 31 years.

One of the Ghosts that Ms. Pate described, the heavyset man wearing a vest and pocket watch, was indeed one of the owners, Bo Clark. She describes a little boy. Well there were two black boys that worked around the theater for my dad, and he let them live in the back of the stage. (My dad was a jack-of-all trades, and did the maintenance and electrical work, even installed the wide screen.) The name she gave was Charlie, but the two boys were Bernard and Ceil. I have a picture taken in 1941 outside the theater on the side by what was Mrs. Zwahlen's newsstand and soda fountain. In the picture are my dad, Emond Clark, the brother of Bo Clark the owner and Bernard and Ceil. Just wondering if Ceil was "Charlie" that she saw.

Yes, there were many times my dad would tell my mom and I about someone talking to him as he checked the house after the theater closed. He would walk through with a flashlight and check each row making sure no one had left a scarf or coat.

There was a young woman named Violet that worked at the theater for many years. I remember one time she was in the ladies' room upstairs and a woman started talking to her. When she came out there was no one around. She went downstairs and asked if a woman had come in or out of the lobby and no one had. (Author's note: The haunted women's rest room once again. This time it's from the 1940s.)

My dad was still the projectionist when he met my mom as she was walking home from school. The next week they got married on dad's supper hour at the courthouse, and she went back with him and sat in the projection room until the theater closed.

When the Majestic Theater was renovated, Dad took over the management of that theater.

I am 70 years young now, and have many memories of the Rialto, as Mom and Dad worked side by side, Mom at the concession stand or in the ticket booth, both at the Rialto and Majestic.

I would love to see a book written about the Rialto as all of my growing up years revolved around this place. I remember that there was an old roll-top desk in the back under the stage where my dad kept his tools and worked. I wonder what ever happened to that desk. Also, he had built a large wooden chest and it was painted black and had his initials "FEO" on it. Frellsen E. Osborne was my dad. Mr. Robb was the other man people would see out front in the lobby; my dad kept the theater running. Good luck on your book.

PS, have you heard about the two black cats that lived in the Rialto, some funny stories about those two. (Author: Black cats and supernatural experiences seem to go together!)

Genie Osborne Williamson

***

Paranormal sighting and smells by Kristin Pope and Roxana Pope: May, 15, 2008:

At 5:30 in the afternoon on May 15, 2008, Kristin and her mother-in-law, Roxana Pope, were touring the theater as part of the open house led by The Spirit Seekers of Arkansas. They left the main auditorium and went down the stairs to beneath the stage where the old vaudeville dressing rooms had been.

While they were there, Kristin noticed a heavy, metal door slowly swing open and then shut. She thought there must be a breeze, but it was deathly still in the area. She mentioned it to her mother-in-law, and, as they both looked, the door swung back open and then closed. It did so two more times until they became spooked and left the room. (Later examination showed the metal door to be on rusty hinges, and opening and closing it cannot be done without some difficulty. Wind could not have moved the door.)

As they walked back out of the basement and up the aisle of the main auditorium, they both smelled a fragrance of something like Ivory soap. It was so strong they stopped and asked each other if they had smelled it. (Was this scent actually perfume?)

2

WEAVING THE TALE

"The boundaries which divide life from death are at best shadowy and vague. Who shall say where one ends, and the other begins?" Edgar Allan Poe

Before we delve into the paranormal occurrences, stories of scandals, and tragic misdeeds in downtown El Dorado, Arkansas, and specifically in and around the Rialto Theater, let us look back at the early history of the town. I believe some of the earliest events that occurred in downtown El Dorado, near the site of the old Rialto Theater, set the stage for what became a concentration of supernatural spirits, bizarre occurrences, and violent acts. After I recorded and documented these various events, I concluded that they are all related.

Why and how this seemingly average, mid-south town, with a current population of around 19,000, collected such a combination of strange, violent characters, macabre incidents, and whispered lore is fascinating. This little piece of South Arkansas—beginning with the controversial and strange naming of the town, to the recent rash of paranormal sighting—has been the stage for some of the most violent and horrific happenings in the United States. When the stories and legends are explored, and the eyewitnesses' stories are added, the history of this town, both present and past, will boggle the imagination.

Just consider a few incidents from this town's violent history, which I will delve into later in more detail: A gunfight on the town square in which three men died and three were wounded—which exactly matches the number of killed and wounded at the Gunfight at the OK. Corral. Then, imagine a gallows just a block away, where horse and hog thieves were hanged as sentences were meted out by vigilante justice. (It was 1912 before the local gallows were abandoned in favor of electrocution by the state.).

And overlooking it all, a theater and downtown packed full of spirits. Now, add to the mix a lawless oil boom with hundreds of murders, and scores of paranormal occurrences, and prepare to have your senses shocked.

The deeper I delved into the paranormal history and tragic events of El Dorado, the more fascinated I became. It seems, that starting with the first settlers, the town produced more stories of unusual, tragic and supernatural events than almost any American town of comparable size.

Of course, as in any accountings of ghosts, paranormal occurrences, and even reports of tragic events by eyewitnesses, absolute facts are hard to come by. This is especially true during the early settlement of the town, when very little of its history or events of the day were documented.

However, when handed-down stories come from independent witnesses over different periods of time, the rumors are laced with numerous eyewitnesses' accounts, and paranormal investigators have gathered hard physical evidence, then the stories take on a solid believability. When all of the events and stores are added up, then the most skeptical listener will nod in agreement, because the old Rialto Theater and the downtown around it are undoubtedly some of the most haunted and historically notorious pieces of real estate in America.

I am a South Arkansas native, who, after graduating from college, worked in Texas and Libya until moving back to El

Dorado in 1975. That's when I began to hear some of the whispered stories that were told concerning the old Rialto Theater and downtown El Dorado. I discounted these stories, since the old theater building does have many creaks and wisps of air that are normal in any building over 50 years old—not to mention being surrounded by a downtown full of ancient buildings that witnessed the unbelievable mayhem of the 1920s oil boom. However, in 2001, an investigative reporter from El Dorado's local newspaper, and his girlfriend, arranged to spend the night in the Rialto Theater, with the goal of disproving any paranormal activity. They abandoned that goal in the wee hours of the morning, after the young couple became terrified by dozens of unexplained noises and strange shadows that suddenly appeared out of nowhere. (Their detailed account of what happened that night is in a later chapter of this book.)

After I read the reporter's account, I started recording every reported unusual event in and around the theater, and I was overwhelmed by the many different and unrelated paranormal reports that patrons and workers told me about, in the old theater as well as the blocks around the theater. Some of these reports came from the theater manager at the time, Ada Williams. Others came from concessions workers, projectionists, and even an electrician who was working on an electrical problem one day. As my file became thicker and thicker with interlaced stories and reports of paranormal activities and lawless behavior, I decided to document as many of these stories as I could.

Along with stories about the spirits who haunt the Rialto and other buildings in downtown El Dorado, there are horrific tales of the town's early days, when the law of the gun and gallows prevailed. And then, just when things were calming down from those lawless days, this little settlement of some 3.800 rather ordinary Southerners experienced a roaring, chaotic oil boom—and the town was never the same.

This collection of documented and rumored accounts, when taken as a whole, is a staggering collection of tragic misdeeds interlaced with tales of ghosts and other spirits. The resulting group of stories forms a clear pattern of supernatural—paranormal activities stretching back some 150 years. In addition, many of these paranormal stories are linked with tragic misdeeds that characterized the early life of this little village. In order to documents these occurrences; I have been assisted by several spirit investigative teams and by Carol Pate, a noted psychic with an international reputation.

Three groups of individuals, from Arkansas and Louisiana, who are known as Spirit Seekers, have investigated the theater, and their findings strongly support the presence of supernatural beings. However, the most vivid account of paranormal activities was documented by Pate. Her vivid descriptions of the various spirits who occupy the old theater and other downtown locations are remarkable and detailed, even down to their names. (An expanded account of her investigation is in a later chapter.)

Pate's credentials are impeccable. She has worked with law enforcement officials to solve many murders and other related crimes, and has been called the foremost psychic in the country. Pate has the ability to not only detect the presence of spirits, but she can also visualize the energy imprints left by individuals. That unique ability has been used to solve numerous criminal investigations.

As my file grew, I began to believe that there were too many reports to discount all of them, and something supernatural must be occurring in the theater and the area around it. As I probed and interviewed, numerous other related events that happened around the theater caught my attention.

Of all the rumors and stories, the most persistent one is about a tunnel connecting the basement of the Rialto Theater to the basement of the Union County Courthouse a block away, and some people say, to the old Presbyterian cemetery a block south. In fact, the tunnel rumors are so persuasive that recently I was told there was an offshoot tunnel from the basement of the Rialto Theater to the basement of the nearby Randolph Hotel.

Somewhere in the dustbin of history—and I will delve into that later in this book—are the rumors of how and why the tunnels were constructed and what might have happened to them. Of course, when I heard these stories, I immediately began to search for the theater entrance of the tunnel, and I found evidence of it beside the stairs that lead to the Rialto basement. One of the spirit investigators crawled into the tunnel some 50 feet, and was stopped by a bricked-up wall.

Obviously, there is a tunnel under the theater, and it undoubtedly was in use at one time. The tunnel runs due north—in the direction of the Union County Courthouse. How far does it extend and what was it used for? And naturally, that leads to the question: Why was it sealed off?

As I investigated further, I heard a flimsy rumor about a tragic accident in the tunnel. Is that why the tunnel was bricked off? Does the tunnel hide a horrific tragedy from prying eyes?

After checking the entrance to the tunnel at the Rialto, we went to the basement of the courthouse where the tunnel was rumored to exit. There I found the entire south basement wall re-plastered. Why? (I've included more details about this bazaar rumor in a later chapter.)

***

At first, I concentrated on paranormal occurrences in the Rialto Theater, but I found out very quickly these were only the tip of the iceberg, spirit-wise. Only a block away is South

Washington Avenue, known as Hamburger Row during the first years of the 1920s oil boom when hamburgers were cooked on open grills out on the sidewalk. That area, just a block south and west of the Rialto, abounds with tales involving the barrelhouses that lined this street. It seems the name "barrelhouse" comes from the old west saloons where drunks were rolled out in whisky barrels when they were drunk and rowdy.

South Washington Avenue, just a block away from the Rialto Theatre, was the lawless, boomtown center of prostitution and gambling. Stories about notorious hijackers, as the robbers and murderers were known, and the hundreds of actual murders committed on Hamburger Row and in the nearby alleyways will curl your hair. Moreover, these murders are factual, and the routes of mortuary wagons that made the pre-dawn rounds to pick up bodies has been documented.

The mayhem of Hamburger Row carried over to the Olympic Billiard Parlor a block away, where Arkansas' most elaborate billiard and domino parlor held court for more than 50 years. Of course, the Randolph Hotel—which was famous (if you want to meet a call girl) or infamous (if you think prostitution is a terrible thing)—stood across the street with its upstairs, mysterious, private Petroleum Club, and its secluded backdoor entrance.

The hotel might not have been a true brothel since it did serve as a regular hotel for many years, but evidence of the so-called "Girls of the Randolph" staying there has spawned a host of rumors that span several generations. And as many will tell you, the "girls" were not fictitious. In fact, till the early 1960s, the buildings around the Rialto Theater on Cedar Street and on South Washington Avenue were home to as many as six houses of prostitution. The last one in The Crystal Hotel closed in 1974.

Of course, all of these buildings were called boarding houses or hotels, but the fact is, they were homes for numerous prostitutes, and they were run by astute madams.

I documented this by an interview with the former night desk clerk of the Garrett Hotel who had worked there during the late 1940s and early 1950s. The Garrett was not one of the houses of ill repute, but in sight of this hotel—less than a block from the Rialto Theater—there were least six so-called hotels or boarding houses where prostitutes resided—and that was in the 1950s!

However, the most shocking story that I uncovered in my research has to do with the first-hand information about a massive graveyard desecration in an old slave cemetery. I was shocked when I heard the account of this event, which had probably occurred during the oil boom of the 1920s when there was virtually no law in certain parts of town. (A later chapter details the horrific act, which has been swept under the rug for decades.)

It seems this area of town, only a block away from the courthouse square, has always been a focal point for the macabre. Early tales of the town's settlement are laced with stories about horse and hog thieves being convicted and led from the courthouse, a block south, to the gallows that were on the corner of Cedar Street and Jefferson Avenue—right across the street from the theater.

Could all of these stories be true? Or could they be the result of imaginations that have amplified half-facts and tied rumors together with flimsy evidence? After I finished collecting the data and stories from this downtown area around the Rialto, I concluded that even though the events described and many of the tales could not be scientifically documented, there was ample evidence that this area of El Dorado has been and still is interlaced with paranormal occurrences. And the tragic incidents described are too vivid, unnerving, and documented to have been faked or imagined.

This area around the downtown square and several blocks south of the square is undoubtedly home to more legends, paranormal occurrences, and intrigue than almost any other locality in the United States. It's not just a haunted theater—it's a haunted downtown and, block-by-block, few places in the country can match the paranormal activities and tales of historic lawlessness found here.

3

DECEPTION

ONE of the most obvious conclusions I came up with during my research has to do with denying the actual, documented past. It is my opinion that a combination of strange circumstances and horrific events occurred in this town's history, and these happenings shocked, warped, and distorted the mindset of many early community leaders. The lawless and sometimes tragic events of El Dorado's past became such an embarrassment to the community that a concentrated effort was made to keep them in the shadows. It was whispered conversation: Not for broadcast or certainly not for publication.

Yes, some of those events that are an integral part of El Dorado's history are still cocktail talk around town. However, if you quiz some of the "old" El Dorado's families—the ones with real knowledge of its history—they'll become uncomfortable, and denials will spring up as they defend the morals of the city. One very elderly citizen said this to me, when I asked about hundreds of <u>documented</u> reports of lawlessness—and <u>murders</u>—during the oil boom of the 1920s:

"No, no, we didn't have any problems during the oil boom. El Dorado has always been a quiet, peaceful town."

Really?

Well, let's take a look at a quote from the local newspaper—and, by the way, this was a small, two-line column on the back page of the Jan. 1, 1922, paper. Remember, the oil boom had been in full swing since Jan. 10, 1921, and during that year, almost 50,000 people had descended upon the city and county. Of that 50,000, a significant number were hardened criminals, petty thieves, and prostitutes.

From a small clip on the back page of the paper: *"It seemed the sport of the night was shooting at church bells. Twelve men were killed."* (From the January 1st, 1922 *El Dorado Daily News*) Ah, yes, you might suspect that many other incidents were ignored, or conveniently swept under the rug so to speak. As I investigated the paranormal incidents in El Dorado and checked into the stories of mayhem and murder, it became more and more apparent that there was an undercurrent of conspiracy that masked many of them. A *"hush, hush, don't talk about it"* **atmosphere** pervaded the culture of the town. And it seems the denial, as I call it, wasn't relegated to community leaders trying to preserve the town's image. No, it was an attitude that penetrated down to the average citizen. My own mother, in a conversation with me, denied active prostitution in the town, though I'm certain she knew better.

During the oil boom and even up into the 1950s, it would be hard to explain why the police, the sheriff's department, and the church leaders—whose churches circled the square— looked the other way as prostitution and gambling flourished. How else would you explain the fact that in the late 1940s and early 1950s as many as six rooming houses or hotels had prostitutes, and their existence was even known by local schoolboys?

So El Dorado was a quiet, peaceful town during the oil boom? No, of course it wasn't. There were so many murders during the first boom years that on Saturday and Sunday mornings before daylight, local mortuary workers drove a wagon down Hamburger Row and the adjacent alleyways—to pick up the bodies. These bodies were kept in the mortuary for 48 hours, and then, if no one claimed them, they were buried in a pauper's cemetery.

Most of these murders were never counted, and, of course, the crimes were never solved. The number of violent deaths can only be estimated, but even a conservative estimate puts them at several thousand. However, if you examine the police reports from the early to mid-1920s, you'll find hardly a mention of these numerous murders.

I interviewed a very elderly man who was a young man during the boom. He told stories about a notorious spot known locally as Death Valley. Several locations have been proposed as the site of the original Death Valley, but this man told me it was located just west of town near the intersection of Hillsboro Street and Timberlane Avenue.

Death Valley was a group of shacks and tents that sprang up near the first oil discovery. The name Death Valley fit the place perfectly. It attracted the lowest of the criminal element, and murders were so frequent that bodies were sometimes just tossed into the small creek that ran through the valley. This gentleman mentioned one of the more interesting facts about the hundreds of murders. *"Almost all of them were done with a knife."*

Witnesses tell of the small creek running red after a Saturday night of mayhem.

Death Valley was at the bottom of a long hill, about a mile west of downtown El Dorado. That little hill, which today seems no more than a slight rise in the land, was a heavily rutted, red clay road in the 1920s. And after a rain it became impassable for automobiles. However, for $3, a team of mules—conveniently stationed at the foot of the hill—would pull your car up the hill.

Just a few hundred yards west of Death Valley stood Pistol Hill, the site of the first oil discovery. There were several barrelhouses across the road from the discovery well, and, according to eyewitnesses, the name Pistol Hill was exactly the right name for this cesspool of lawlessness.

It seemed, the deeper I delved into the unusual, sometimes violent, history of the community, the more bizarre the stories. Of course, denial runs deep in El Dorado and confirmation of the legends, stories, and events in this town's actual history have been hard to come by. In my research through records, newspaper accounts, and oral history, I ran across literally dozens of individuals who refused to divulge the names or even confirm that certain events actually happened. However, I was able to substantiate many of the stories by the multiplicity of accounts—some of which were later denied.

As I collected these stories of events from the past, the period when something occurred, (as described by different individual) seemed to overlap and even skip from one generation to the next. I'm sure that some of the stories I recorded are incorrect in the time-line of the city, but according to numerous oral accounts, these events actually occurred—maybe in the oil boom of the '20s instead of the Depression. But, because these anecdotes have been recounted by so many individuals, I believed they did happen.

As I interviewed person after person, the stories about El Dorado's past became stranger. Many individuals, who were eyewitnesses to some of the horrific happenings, when questioned further, suddenly became mute and frowns replaced smiles when I asked for details. And if I asked for corroboration, many times I got either silence or long-winded out-and-out lies about a peaceful, quiet, and reverent early El Dorado.

Of course, as it concerns quiet and reverent flies in the face of factual accounts that have documented the thousands of murders. Violence, however, did not begin during the oil boom. It started in the town's earliest history and exploded during the 1920s boom where violence went off-scale.

I decided it would be my task, when I decided to write this book, to record, and if possible, document every story, legend, scoundrel, and paranormal event that I could come up with. Of course, many of these handed-down stories are just that—stories with no basis in fact. But many others are eyewitness accounts.

I have not attempted to sort fact from lore or legend. If I did, this account of the strange and violent acts of the past would be an incomplete record of El Dorado's history. However, most of the rumors and accounts that I have included in this book have multiple sources.

In other words, my attitude was not to distinguish between rumors, eyewitness accounts, and flimsy guesswork with little hard evidence, but to let you, the reader, discern the truth. As you read this book, I think you'll find this little Southern village has an astonishing history.

So, I have made it my job to give readers a basis for their decision. I have expanded and included as much data and information as possible, and in order to bring to life some of the events of the past, I have inserted possible dialogue that is purely from my imagination. However, I think that by doing so, readers will have a better feel for the events that make up El Dorado's history.

The earliest accounts of the town's history, dating from the 1840s, consists of rumors and stories that sometimes contradict each other, but since most of the early history of El Dorado is passed-down lore with a good dose of fiction, it's not unlikely that the town's oral history would be incongruous.

The first stories, beginning in the early 1840s, are from the first settlers of the community, and, as you will note, El Dorado, from its very beginning, was unlike any of the other small towns in the mid-South. Naturally, since many of the events that occurred during the settlement of the town were never recorded, much of this early history has been handed down from generation to generation. And while much of it would fall into the category of rumor or folklore, there is common threads that tie many of these stories together.

4

SCARBOROUGH'S LANDING OR CHAMPAGNOLLE LANDING OR... 'EL DORADO'

THE original county seat of Union County was Champagnolle Landing (later called Scarborough's Landing and then renamed Champagnolle Landing) on the nearby Ouachita River. In the early 1840s it was a Yellow Fever infested, rundown, former French trading post supposedly founded by Pedro Champagnolle.

Actually, Champagnolle was probably not really Pedro's last name. Pedro was from Champagnolle, France, and he named his trading post after his hometown. He was a French fur traders who illegally traded with the Indians during the 1770s. (As a side note: While the Louisiana Purchase was under Spanish control in 1774, the Spanish Commandant, Athanase de Mezieres, rounded up "vagabonds" from the upper Ouachita River area. He deported 14 people, one of whom was Pedro Champagnolle.)

Yes, the very earliest reports from what would someday be Union County began with stories of criminal activity. Evidently, Pedro and other French fur traders had been in and out of what would one day be South Arkansas for some 30 years before American settlers began to arrive in the area. When the first settlers came, they found several small settlements along the Ouachita River, and almost all of the streams and prominent landscape features already named by the French.

When Hunter and Dunbar, a Lewis and Clark type expedition, came up the Ouachita River in 1804, the river was already named "Ouachita," the high bluff on the river was called

"Cote de Champagnolle," (Champagnolle Bluff) and the stream a mile up the river, Champagnolle Creek.

Evidently, some years later, around 1825, one of the early English settlers, not happy with the French name, renamed the river port Scarborough's Landing—after himself. Of course, the local Native Americans had already named everything, but very few of the Indian names have survived. About the only Indian name remaining is the "Ouachita" River. The Ouachita Indians named it. "The River of the Ouachitas."

One of the few French names that has survived over time is the name Champagnolle. It was originally a fur trading camp and a meeting place, where the French traded with the Caddo and Ouachita Indians. In 1846 when the county seat of Union County was moved from Echore Fabre (modern-day Camden) to Scarborough's Landing, the settlement reverted to its original name, Champagnolle.

The largest Indian village, in what is now South Arkansas, was just a few miles up the river from Champagnolle Landing. The village was established about a mile away from the river to get out of the flood plain of the stream. This Indian village, which today carries the name of "Boone's Mound" covered a large area and had several ceremonial mounds. It was located on the bank of a large creek that Pedro renamed Champagnolle. The Indian village was the largest settlement in South Arkansas for hundreds of years, but abandoned during the mid-1800s when the Indians were moved to reservations in Oklahoma.

The initial Anglo population of Champagnolle Landing was mainly a corrupt and dangerous group of illegal French trappers, mixed-blood Caddo and Ouachita Indians, renegades on the run from Fort Miro or New Orleans, and a small smattering of English settlers. It was a community that, according to accounts by travelers through Arkansas during the early 1800s, wasn't fit for man nor dog.

The small village consisted of a hotel, a couple of general stores, and four saloons: Two saloons were on the south side of the Ouachita River, and another two across the river in Hogskin County. Evidently, even as lawless as Champagnolle Landing was, across the river in another county was a safer place to reside. That is, if you were running from the law or stealing hogs, as many of the early settlers were. The village had upper and lower sections much like Natchez, Mississippi, and Champagnolle.

"Under the Hill" was not much more than a den of thieves who preyed off the riverboat traffic and any unarmed men who might venture down the hill after dark.

During the mid 1830s, when English settlers from Mississippi and Alabama moved west by riverboat, the first settlement north of Fort Miro was Champagnolle Landing or Scarborough's Landing. The former French fur trading post had a population of fewer than 100. Another French fur trading post, Echore Fabre, was about 30 miles up the river, and in the early 1800s, these two trading posts made up about 90 percent of the population of the county.

By 1845, both trading posts had become small villages, and American settlers from Mississippi and Alabama were scattered throughout South Arkansas. However, the overall population in the area was still fewer than a couple of thousand.

As the English settlers arrived at Echore Fabre, they weren't about to live in a town with a French name, so they changed the name of Echore Fabre to Camden. However, for some reason, the name Champagnolle Landing remained, (even after going through the name change to Scarborough's Landing). Even today several streets in South Arkansas and a large creek bare that name.

Accounts from the small village of Champagnolle Landing, which was situated on the highest river bluff north of Fort Moro, are scattered, but considering the Yellow Fever epidemic that gripped the little settlement every summer, it must have been a grim place to live. A scattering of lean-tos, dirt floor cabins, and log buildings made up most of the structures in Champagnolle Under the Hill. Since the Under the Hill town flooded every spring, permanent structures didn't exist.

The Upper Champagnolle town boasted several substantial buildings and gave the small village a semblance of a small rural settlement. One of the early English settlers by the name of Albert Rust became a Confederate general and gave the little settlement the distinction of being the smallest town in the south to produce a general. The only benefit to living in Champagnolle Landing was to be near the Ouachita River, where there was an abundance of game. The locally famous Passenger Pigeon roost made for prime hunting.

Today the abandoned town area still carries the name Champagnolle, and the old Passenger Pigeon roost farther down the river is still called Pigeon Hill. Stories abound about Passenger Pigeons by the millions roosting in the virgin Beech trees along the ridge. In the fall, thousands of barrels of salted pigeons were shipped south to New Orleans.

Many pigeons may have been in and around the little village of Champagnolle, but, by all accounts, proper women were in short supply. The riverboats that came upriver from New Orleans bringing supplies in the 1800s, also brought the first prostitutes into the state. Naturally, they stayed in Champagnolle Under the Hill.

In the early 1840s there was a consensus to move the county seat to a more central location. They did, and named the new county seat, El Dorado. Huh? El Dorado? Where on earth did they come up with that name?

Stories abound about the naming of El Dorado, and the two that are the most prevalent are that the town named for a brand of Tequila and a Saloon, or that the moniker came from the "black gold" (oil) that arrived some 70-years later.

The correct answer is clouded in a veil of history. But let's look at the facts. The name "El Dorado" in Spanish means "The Golden," and supposedly the town was named by the four men who surveyed the town site. These men had the task of picking a new county seat; relocating the county seat from Champagnolle Landing on the Ouachita River—away from Yellow Fever and mosquito-infested swamps—to a more central spot in the county on high ground, with a good water source.

Their search took them to the site of the present-day courthouse. In the 1840s, this particular piece of land was covered in virgin timber, and a large spring and pond occupied the spot where the courthouse now stands. The site, with its good water, high ground, and central location, fit the criteria for a new county seat. The spot where the courthouse now stands is almost in the center of Union County and is one of the highest points in the county. That, combined with the large spring for drinking water, sealed the selection. The men came away convinced that the new county seat should be at that location, and the name of the settlement should be El Dorado.

But, really, how on earth did these men decide to name a town in the mid-South El Dorado? Doesn't that strike you as unusual for a town deep in the piney woods of South Arkansas to have a Spanish name? There were no Spanish settlers in the state at that time, only English mixed with a few leftover French from the early frontier days.

In California, New Mexico, or even West Texas, El Dorado is common because of the Spanish influence. But in South Arkansas in 1845? I think not. Where on earth did these men come up with the name El Dorado?

Of course, there's a romantic piece of folklore—and it is strictly hearsay—about how the four-man committee came up with that name. Yes, according to lore, these "visionaries" noted that one of the springs located near where the Union County Courthouse now stands formed a pond that was large enough to attract ducks in the fall. This would be the site for the new county seat of Union County.

According to this fanciful story, the men sat down on a log near the pond, and, while they rested, they discussed the new town's name. Our local historians have a handed-down account of one of the men having a vision about golden riches that would someday make the little town rich and famous. Evidently, his imagination was so vivid that he convinced the other men to name the town after the riches that would soon follow.

When the romantic, exotic name of El Dorado was mentioned, the men agreed: "El Dorado" would be the name of the new county seat. No these four men weren't from Oz, and as unlikely as the story seems to be, it has been told over and over until it's stated as fact. The truth of the matter is that it is a total fabrication made up by a generation who wanted El Dorado to be free of any blemishes associated with its past.

The fact is that these men were English settlers, and with the animosity toward the Spanish at that time, they would have never used a Spanish name—unless the spot, which already had settlers living there, was known as **the El Dorado...Saloon.**

Of course, some of local historians still assert that the vision or dream that one of the men had was an insight into the black gold (oil) that would someday—some +80 years down the road—make the little town live up to its name. And, of course, that was before the discovery of oil in the United States.

Really? I know you're saying, "You've got to be kidding!"

Yes, that is the official version. A little hard to believe isn't it? Trying to link gold or oil to a piney woods, mid-South town requires you to separate logic from your thought process. However, it seems there is a more believable, whispered story, that has a lot more credibility, but it's not a story you will ever hear from any of El Dorado's keepers of its history. Here is one of account of the founding of El Dorado, and how the little village received its name.

The story begins in the fall of 1840 when one of the county's early settlers, a peddler named Mathew Rainey, stopped at a spring that is now the center of downtown El Dorado. His wagon had a broken wheel, and he stopped to repair the wheel. (Everyone agrees with this first part of the story.)

The job took several days, and while he was repairing the wagon, farmers from around the county came by, and Rainey sold almost all of his merchandise—much of which was apparently whiskey, according to early records. Encouraged by the brisk business, he set up a small, one-room store constructed from logs and arranged for merchandise to come up the river from New Orleans. And, as his business prospered, Rainey added a saloon with a dirt floor attached to the back of the store. (Of course, the saloon is not in the "official" version—bad idea to have a saloon in the official history of the town.)

According to local sources, his saloon became very popular and after running low on bourbon because of erratic riverboat arrivals, Rainey stocked his bar with tequila, purchased at a discount from another peddler who had come from Texas hauling a load of Tequila. The peddler, who feared he would be stuck with a load of tequila in an area where bourbon whiskey was the preferred drink, made Rainey a good deal on the tequila and the saloon-owner purchased the entire wagonload.

When Rainey unloaded the tequila, he noted that the golden-colored liquor was named El Dorado Tequila, which translated means The Golden Tequila (probably a cheap Patrón-type knockoff that maintained its golden color), So Rainey reportedly named the saloon after the tequila. At that point, Rainey's Store became The El Dorado Saloon.

It was a few years later that county commissioners began discussions about moving the county seat from Champagnolle Landing, on the Ouachita River, to a higher place in the county, away from the river and yellow fever. And they sent the four-man group of scouts to find a site for the new county seat.

Reports indicate that the men knew right where to go, and instead of investigating other sites in the area, they went straight to the El Dorado Saloon. After drinking all night, they decided to move the county seat to the area around Rainey's store. (Actually, even the four men picking the site and coming up with the name El Dorado is just folklore.) I'm sure everyone living in Champagnolle Landing and the rest of Union County were already familiar with Rainey's store and saloon and already called the place El Dorado.

Of course, Rainey wanted to name the new town Raineyville, but since everyone in the county already called the place El Dorado, after the saloon, this became the official name of the little settlement. Initially, a few of the settlers tried to pronounce El Dorado properly (like the car), but the overwhelming English majority drawled the name until it came to be pronounced, "El Do-ray-da."

Well, maybe that story is just another tale. But it sure seems a lot more logical to believe this than a story about uneducated, country folks naming the town after a vision of "black gold," when it would be decades before the first oil well was drilled in the Union County, and 15 years before the first oil well was drilled in North America. And to top it off, would the founders have named the town a word they couldn't even pronounce or knew the meaning of?

The county commissioners approved the site for the new county seat and soon the duck pond was filled and a temporary log courthouse was thrown up. Justice was uneven at best, and since there were no jails south of Little Rock, many times justice meant the lawbreakers were executed instead of being taken to Little Rock for incarceration.

The stories of horse and pig thieves being hanged is part of the local history of this little village. In fact, the county across the Ouachita River, Calhoun Country, is still nicknamed "Hogskin County" from the early days when hog thieves from Union County carried stolen hogs across the river to skin them. Would they really hang a man for stealing a hog? You bet they would and did—many times. Don't forget this happened in the 1840s, in the backwoods of South Arkansas—not New York State.

5

THE GALLOWS

IT seems, that after an unusually severe season of Yellow Fever, the county leaders decided the proximity to the river seemed to increase the risk of contracting the disease. Of course, they didn't understand mosquitoes were responsible for Yellow Fever. Instead, they used "Arkansas Logic" and blamed "bad air" from the surrounding swamps. That was the reason they voted to move the county seat to higher ground away from the river—and the "bad air."

However, according to some sources, there were other reasons to move the county seat from Champagnolle Landing. By 1845, assorted vagrants on the run from the law, part-time French trappers, New Orleans prostitutes, and other assorted riffraff made up a goodly portion of the settlement's population. These early settlers created a slum-like situation that made up most of Champagnolle Under the Hill. Newly arriving English settlers all settled in the upper village, However, with all the squalor in the Under the Hill part of Champagnolle, moving the county seat away from the corruption and slum-like area on the river, seem like a good idea.

The distasteful living conditions in Champagnolle Landing and Under the Hill was the real reason to move the county seat. A new town in the center of the county—a new county seat—was a better way to attract new settlers.

However, as soon as El Dorado's town lots were staked, most of this assorted riffraff of settlers, prostitutes, and vagrants from both Under the Hill and Upper Champagnolle walked the 10 miles from Champagnolle Landing and descended on the little community of El Dorado like the plague. Of course, that rowdy bunch only added to the mix of characters from other parts of the large county, who had already arrived, attracted by the El Dorado Saloon.

It was an extremely shady start for a town, but instead of tossing out the criminal element, who came from Champagnolle Landing Under the Hill to drink in the saloon and cavort with the prostitutes, the town accepted them, and the little village began to grow. As El Dorado gained population, its rowdy reputation was further tainted by the rumored accounts of frontier and sometimes vigilante justice that occurred during the early settlement days.

When the town was incorporated, neither the town nor the county had a jail, and it was commonplace to hang convicted criminals rather than send them north to Little Rock for incarceration. According to early accounts, many criminals were executed by being hanged from a limb on a massive oak tree a block south of El Dorado's first courthouse on a lot across the street from what is now the Rialto Theater. It seems many times the trials were only a step away from vigilante justice.

The original Union County Courthouse was a crude log structure built on the edge of a big spring and duck pond, very close to where the current courthouse now stands. As the town grew, the sheriff, who wanted something more secure than the limb of an oak tree to execute criminals, contracted a local carpenter to build an official gallows. The new gallows was 100 feet from the south line of the original town lot and 30 feet from the east line.

This location, which was a barren, just-cleared quarter of a city block, would become the corner of Cedar Street and Jefferson Avenue. According to accounts, the poorly constructed, makeshift gallows was prone to malfunctioning. The lot where the gallows was located is immediately across from the Rialto Theater—some 50 feet north of the bronze statues in the current Oil Heritage Park.

Recently, I interviewed a woman who offered collaboration of the gallows. In fact, she added a bit of possible racist lore to the presence of the gallows. It seems not only were the gallows used to hang individuals from Union County, but, according to this elderly woman's grandmother, authorities from Hampton, the county seat of Calhoun "Hogskin" County, also sent prisoners to El Dorado to be executed.

One particular prisoner was a black man accused of raping a white woman, and it seems the evidence was largely circumstantial. The man was probably innocent, but the sheriff wanted the man officially executed instead of being strung up by a Hampton lynch mob. The sheriff in El Dorado was happy to accommodate, and the man was promptly hanged.

Executions started shortly after the town was incorporated and continued until 1912. During this era of the state's history, each county executed convicted criminals by hanging them in the county where the crime was committed. That changed in 1912 when the governor signed a bill making electrocution the official manner in which to carry out the death penalty; executions were then carried out in one of the state's prisons.

There are many accounts of horse thieves and other criminals being hanged on these gallows after a hurried, sometimes vigilante trial. Because of the remote, frontier nature of the early settlement, there wasn't always a judge present, and the dispensation of justice was anything but evenhanded. The whispered accounts of these executions sometime trended toward the macabre, with sloppy work by the part-time hangman, who caused protracted deaths

Early reports from the mid-1840s, soon after the town was incorporated, are sketchy, but many of these accounts of frequent hangings have been handed down and repeated by some of older residents of the city, as being told to them by their great-grandparents. The only remaining piece of history from this period is a 6-foot long, perfectly preserved, concrete, horse-watering trough a block away from the site of the gallows.

During the early days of the community, horse-watering troughs were placed on most of the blocks in the downtown area. There is the only one left. It sits on Hill Avenue about two blocks from the gallows. The watering trough is still intact after almost 160 years—waiting on another thirsty horse, or maybe it's there as a reminder of the violent frontier heritage that marked the town's early days.

(This story was told to me by a longtime resident of Union County. It was passed on to him by his grandfather.)

This tale, which dates back to the mid-1840s, has to do with one of the horse-watering troughs. It seems, after a quick trial, the judge ordered a man, who had confessed to stealing a cow, to be hanged. As the condemned prisoner walked toward the gallows from the courthouse, he tried to escape. According to the story about the escape, the condemned prisoner hit the sheriff with his handcuffed hands, knocked him down, and then ran down what is now Jefferson Avenue.

The sheriff jumped to his feet, pulled out his revolver, and then pursued him with several other men. The sheriff fired at the man with his single-shot revolver but missed, and it seemed the prisoner might escape. The prisoner dashed down the street toward a wooded area about the time a hunter named Tom Pinson came walking up Jefferson Avenue. He had just returned to town from a bird hunt, and was heading toward the courthouse.

"Tom! Stop that man!—Shoot, the son-of-a-bitch!" screamed the sheriff.

About that time the escaped prisoner dashed past Tom, who was armed with a double-barreled shotgun filled with birdshot. He hesitated for a few seconds, but then raised his shotgun and sent both barrels of birdshot into the back of the fleeing prisoner. There was an ear-piercing scream, and the force of both barrels of birdshot sent the condemned man sprawling forward beside a concrete horse-watering trough. He was bleeding from dozens of pieces of birdshot, but wasn't mortally wounded. The sheriff and the men that had been chasing him arrived before he could regain his feet and two men grabbed and held him for the sheriff.

"By God, you thought you was gonna get away, didn't you?—Thanks Tom. Damn, you really peppered his ass!—Okay, boys, let's take the sorry bastard over to the gallows and noose 'em up."

The prisoner, who was in terrible pain, was bleeding profusely from at least 50 puncture wounds made by the small birdshot. Blood had soaked his shirt and was running down both arms. He was screaming, still trying to run, and it was all two men could do to control him.

"Hell, Sheriff, I ain't gonna hang 'em till you cleans 'em up. I ain't about to get blood all over me trying to put on the noose and hood," said the hangman, who had run along with the sheriff as they chased the prisoner.

The sheriff stood there a minute and then, as he looked at the horse-watering trough, he nodded his head.

"Boys," he said to the two men holding the prisoner, *"dip the sorry bastard in that horse-watering trough to clean 'em up and hold him under till he gets real quiet."*

There was a nod of understanding and the two men yanked the prisoner over to the watering trough. Then, with a man on each arm, they shoved him to the bottom of the trough and held him there. A couple of minutes passed and the prisoner stopped struggling.

"All right, boys, I believe y'all has calmed him down and washed him up enough for J. B. to hang 'em."

The men carried the condemned man up the street to the gallows where the hangman hanged a lifeless prisoner. They left the horse-watering trough with its water stained red. And according to the story, later that day the trough was drained, cleaned, and refilled.

However, soon the water turned red again and the process was repeated. After several more tries the trough was emptied and as superstition abounded in the little town, a hole was cut in the bottom to keep water from standing in it, and the watering trough was abandoned.

I guess the question is: After 164 years, will the water still turn red if the trough is repaired and filled? Maybe. The concrete trough is still sitting where it was originally placed with a hole cut in the bottom to keep water from standing. Stories have continued to this day about the watering trough that won't hold clear water. Did the condemned man who was drowned in the trough cause this? Are the dark, rust-colored stains on the bottom of the trough a reminder of what happened back in the 1840s? But maybe there're not rust stains at all... but bloodstains.

More importantly, do the ghosts of the condemned prisoner and all the other executed men, still haunt the site? Is the old gallows area, where so many men were executed without a trial, home to spirits that still roam the back alleys and streets seeking justice? I believe, as we delve into the paranormal occurrences reported on and around this small track of land, we will agree something spiritual or ghost-like is happening on those moonless nights when a deathly stillness hangs over the area, and the glimmering of energy orbs dot the back alleyways.

In my investigation, I have concluded that most of the time, spirits occupy a building or an area after tragic events occur. Certainly, with so many men executed after vigilante trials, there is good reason to believe their spirits are present, and they are making themselves known. Knowing the circumstances of these early lawless days, it would be unusual if spirits were not present. Some individuals also point back to El Dorado's rough-and-tumble founding and the gallows as the cause of the unusual activities around the old theater and in the nearby alleys. Are these the spirits of men who were unjustly executed and are still roaming the alleyways and back streets protesting their innocence? *Are they the ghosts of the gallows?*

That question has never been satisfactory answered, but reports of paranormal activities in the back-alleys and streets around the theater abound, and it makes sense that the horrific events that occurred in the past would have resulted in some these activities.

The story about the old horse-watering trough has been hidden away and swept under the carpet by "old" El Dorado families. It is considered an embarrassment, and that and other stories of El Dorado's lawless frontier days reside in the dustbin of history… along with many other shadowy happenings.

6

BLOOD ON DIRT STREETS

AFTER the founding of El Dorado in the mid-1840s, the town grew to about 2,500 by the time the Civil War began. Records show that 1,500 men from Union County marched off to fight for the Confederacy and only 500 returned. Reconstruction and recovery from the war was slow, but by the turn of the century, the town had resumed its growth and there was a growing sense that prosperity was returning to Union County.

As merchants and businessmen built the first brick buildings around the courthouse, however, there was an increasing amount of animosity that pitted some of the older more established merchants and businessmen against the newer entrepreneurs who had previously been county farmers.

The early history of El Dorado had several exclamation points as the town experienced steady growth. One of these highlights—or what some senior citizens call lowlights—of El Dorado concerns a violent gunfight that occurred a block north of the Rialto Theater on the east side of the courthouse. The gunfight, or as it is known from recent publicity, Showdown at Sunset, resulted in the death of three men and the wounding of three others—exactly the same number of casualties as the famous *Gunfight at the OK Corral*, in Tombstone, Arizona.

The gunfight occurred at the intersection of Main Street and Jefferson Avenue, a block north of the Rialto Theater, on the courthouse square—the heart of downtown El Dorado. The original town records indicate that across from the east side of the courthouse, the first buildings were erected after the village of El Dorado was incorporated.

In 1845, this site, across from the courthouse, housed a large, wood-framed general store and saloon called the El Dorado. A number of years later the general store and saloon were razed and the Arcade Hotel and Union Dry Goods businesses occupied this spot. Several decades later a Safeway grocery store and a McCrory's five-and-dime store were located there, and in 1987 the old fire-gutted shell of the McCrory's Building was leveled and the current building, the Corinne Building, was erected.

To understand why two groups of leading citizens of the community would engage in a violent gunfight, we must consider the early history of the city. We know horse, pig, and cattle rustlers were hanged on the gallows just south of the courthouse square. Adding to the propensity for violence were the Confederate Soldiers from Union County, who marched down Main Street on their way to the front in Northern Virginia, or to join forces with General (Joseph) Johnston's Army of Tennessee.

The 500 soldiers who returned to Union County had been through the most violent war our nation's history, and, as veterans of a bloody conflict, they saw differences settled by gunfire. It was a time when a challenge to a man's honor was met with violence.

After El Dorado recovered from the War and the terrible, repressive Reconstruction, the town began to prosper and with the contribution from the timber and farming industry, the population steadily grew. However, the community was still considered on the edge of the frontier, and the frontier attitude of "take justice into your own hands" still prevailed.

It was only 37 years after the end of the Civil War when this frontier code of honor was challenged.

On Oct. 9th, 1902, at 4:40 p.m., one of the most violent episodes in El Dorado's history occurred on Jefferson Avenue, right in front of the courthouse. An argument between the Parnell family of downtown businessmen and Marshal Guy B. Tucker (grandfather of former Arkansas Gov. Jim Guy Tucker) reached the boiling point. After a slur (which no one would admit uttering) aimed at the Parnell family's honor, a horrific gunfight took place.

From all accounts, the bad blood between the Parnell family—consisting of Old Man Parnell, as he was called, by his eight sons, and a group of downtown businessmen who had aligned themselves with City Marshal Tucker—had been building for several months. The Parnell family, poor farmers eking out a living on a small farm southwest of El Dorado, had moved into town and had recently opened two downtown stores. Apparently, because of jealousy or maybe retail competition, the Parnell brothers and several downtown businessmen had words over everything from the Parnells' business practices to construction of a sidewalk beside one of the Parnells' stores.

According to several sources, the wooden sidewalk had a loading dock extending over the sidewalk, which made it difficult to travel down the sidewalk without walking out in the street. Marshal Tucker had been by the Parnell store earlier in the day, and had told the Parnells to remove the loading dock from the sidewalk.

That was the final straw for the Parnells, who believed several downtown businessmen had encouraged City Marshal Tucker to take action against the loading dock. This seemly small matter became the lightning rod for the Parnell resentment. By all accounts strong words had been spoken over the weeks before the gunfight. However, there was a beautiful, red-haired woman who was the fuse that ignited the fight. That lady was Miss Jessie Stevenson, a local photographer's assistant.

The photographer Bob Mullens, a good friend of the Parnell family, had fallen in love with the beautiful Miss Jessie, his assistant, and soon he was professing his love and actively pursuing her. However, Miss Jessie was engaged to a young man from Texarkana, and she rejected Mullens' advances. Mullens persisted, and when he refused to leave her alone, Miss Jessie complained to Marshal Tucker.

The Marshal warned Mullens not to bother Miss Jessie again, but by all accounts Mullen continued. Evidently, the situation became tense; Miss Jessie feared for her safety and decided to leave town and go to Texarkana to be with her fiancé.

Mullens found out that she was on the train, and rushed to catch the train before it left town. Someone apprised Marshal Tucker about the situation, and he and Constable Harrison Dearing rode on horseback west following the train. Since the train stopped at every small town along the way, the men managed to catch the train at a small town west of El Dorado, where they arrested Bob Mullens.

On the way back to El Dorado, an altercation ensued with Mullens and Marshal Tucker shot and killed him. The Parnells claimed Tucker executed Mullens because he was a friend of theirs, and the next day the Parnells demanded that Tucker be arrested. But the Marshal was not arrested and never charged. Marshal Tucker maintained he had shot Mullens because he was trying to escape.

Only a few days had passed after Bob Mullens was killed, when the loading dock complaint surfaced again. It was the final straw. Marshal Tucker ordered the dock to be removed from the sidewalk, but the Parnells contended similar conditions existed all over town and that other merchants where allowed to do what they were being forbidden to do.

One Thursday afternoon, three of the Parnell brothers walked up Jefferson Avenue to challenge Marshal Tucker's authority to remove the loading dock. At about 4 p.m. that October afternoon, on a dirt street in front of the old, redbrick Victorian courthouse, the Parnell brothers called out Marshal Tucker.

"Tucker, come out here and talk to us!" Mat Parnell yelled. In a few minutes, Marshal Tucker walked to the doorway and Mat Parnell yelled again.

"Tucker, we've had it with you telling us how to run our business. You need to do some explainin'," hollered Mat.

"Mat, you and your brothers had better get on back home. I don't have to explain anything to you. Now, don't cause any trouble or you'll damn sure regret it."

A wrought iron fence surrounded the courthouse, and as the intensity of the threatening increased, Constable Harrison Dearing joined Marshal Tucker. The Parnells were on the street side of the wrought-iron fence and Marshal Tucker and Harrison Dearing were on the courthouse side. Constable Dearing was a good friend of the Parnells, and he tried to calm things down.

"Now, Mat you and Jim need to calm down and come back tomorrow, and we'll see what we can do to make this situation right," said Dearing. It seemed as if he had convinced the Parnells to leave, but just as they turned away to leave, a slur was shouted at them. To this day no one knows who yelled it.

"Slink away, you yellow-bellied cowards!"

The Parnells turned with their pistols drawn, and all hell broke loose.

There have been many conflicting accounts about exactly what happened in those few minutes when Marshal Tucker walked out to confront the Parnell brothers. Who fired the first shot, who yelled the slur, and if Marshal Tucker shot one of the

Parnells in the back. The following sworn testimony taken by a grand jury is from one of the participants, Jim Parnell.

"I saw the fighting in which my brothers were killed. When I came up, I heard Tucker say that we were a set of cowardly sons-of-bitches and Tucker turned his gun on me and fired. The shooting became general. When Tucker shot at me the second time, I got behind the courthouse fence gatepost. When the smoke cleared away, Dearing and Walter were dead. Tom and Tucker were in a scuffle over a gun. Mat came in to stop him. Dr. Tucker, the Marshal's brother, and Dr. Hilton ran up to Mat and one of them stabbed him in the back and the other shot at him. Mat got hold of the pistol. I ran up and knocked Hilton down, just as he was about to shoot Mat Parnell. The pistol fired and dropped from his hand, and he left and went across the street. Frank Newton, just about the time I saw Hilton and Dr. Tucker scuffling with Mat, ran up and shot Tom in the back. As I went to Mat, Newton shot several shots at either Mat or myself. He shot holes in my hat and clothes. Guy Tucker was pulled loose from Tom and as Tom started staggering across the street Tucker shot him again in the back. (Tom fell and died on the dirt street in front of the Arcade Hotel.) *After I knocked Hilton off of Mat, I left and did not return to the scene of the shooting."*

Signed, Jim Parnell, July 3rd, 1902.

Sheriff H. C. Norris rushed out of the courthouse and managed to stop the gunfight, but three men were killed and another three seriously wounded late that October afternoon in front of the Union County Courthouse. Marshal Tucker had six gunshot wounds, but none of them were life-threatening.

El Dorado was still a growing town and its streets were dirt, mixed with a little gravel. It would take a "pave-the-street campaign" several years later, led by newspaper owner George Mason, to put in concrete streets around the courthouse.

That October afternoon, the blood of these six men stained the dirt street so much that a cleanup crew had to be dispatched by the mayor to dig up the bloodstained dirt and carry it off for disposal. According to some accounts, the men hauled away several wheelbarrows full of this dirt and dumped it a block south on a vacant lot—near where the old gallows had been located. Later that afternoon, the bloodstained dirt of six men was scattered on the vacant lot behind the gallows site.

It is no wonder—considering the numerous men who had been hanged and add the blood of six more men added to the mix—that numerous people have seen evidence of paranormal energy there, and have heard strange sounds in the back alleys behind the buildings that line Main Street, adjacent to Oil Heritage Park.

Are the spirits that psychic Carol Pate recognized in an around the site of the gallows and in the alleyways, the spirits of the men who were gunned down that October day or were hanged on the gallows after vigilante trials? Certainly, a logical conclusion would say: Yes.

7

THE BLOODY AFTERMATH OF THE GUNFIGHT

MARSHAL Tucker was wounded, but he recovered and resumed his job as El Dorado's City Marshal. However, the feud had just started. Within a few weeks after the courthouse gunfight, several men on both sides were ambushed and killed. The tension grew and about a year after the courthouse gunfight, Marshal Tucker met John Parnell on a downtown street. They had words, and, according to eyewitnesses, Marshal Tucker pulled his gun, shot, and killed the unarmed man. Another man's blood had stained a dirt street in downtown El Dorado.

Marshal Tucker was arrested and charged with murder. However, the Marshal was not about to have his fate put in the hands of a rural South Arkansas attorney. He hired a savvy lawyer from Little Rock, and, after a lengthy trial in which Tucker claimed John Parnell was reaching in his pocket seemingly for a gun, Marshal Tucker was found innocent.

However, he was stripped of his job, and in 1903 former Marshal Guy B. Tucker moved back to Champagnolle, Arkansas, or Champagnolle Landing as it was known. Champagnolle was the first county seat of Union County, and some the dregs of South Arkansas still lived there in lower Champagnolle Under the Hill along the river. Tucker had grown up there, where his parents taught school.

Marshal Tucker and his family actually lived in a small community called Upper Champagnolle about a mile up the river from Champagnolle Landing. Tucker went to work tending bar in the MinkEye Saloon across the river in Calhoun County. By all accounts, considering the stories from the backwoods of South Arkansas, the MinkEye was a rough place, built of logs, with bare rooms for travelers to stay the night and only a lantern for light. Marshal Tucker tended bar, took in travelers, and even cleaned up each night after closing.

The MinkEye would usually close right before sunset, and Marshal Tucker would walk to the ferry and re-cross the river back to Champagnolle Landing. On many occasions, his 11-year-old son, James Guy Tucker, would ride out on horseback from the family farm at Upper Champagnolle to pick up his father.

On June 6, 1903, young James Guy Tucker picked up his father and together they rode to Champagnolle Landing and picked up their mail. As they left town, riding along a shadowy river trail to their farm, they were stopped by former Sheriff H. C. Norris, the lawman who had stopped the original gunfight with the Parnells.

As the two talked, a gunshot rang out and Tucker was hit in the left arm, breaking it. Another shot hit Tucker in the chest, and two gunmen rode away while Norris attended to the wounded Tucker.

Of course, some questions immediately come to mind: What was H. C. Norris doing on that remote road in the first place? And why did he stop former Marshal Tucker at exactly the place of ambush? Was it to allow the bushwhackers to have a stationary shot as they ambushed Tucker? And why did former Sheriff Norris not even attempt to return fire or apprehend the men who fired on Tucker?

It is my opinion that that Norris was working with the men who ambushed Tucker. It is too unlikely for the ambush to have happened exactly where Norris stopped Tucker.

Marshal Tucker recovered from his wounds, but lost the arm broken by the first bullet. After the attempt on his life, Tucker left Union County and moved to Little Rock where he became a very successful politician. His grandson, Jim Guy Tucker, was elected lieutenant governor of Arkansas in 1990, and when Gov. Bill Clinton was elected President in 1992, Jim Guy Tucker became governor.

According to lore and legends, the tragic deaths of the three men killed in the actual gunfight was only the first of numerous deaths related to the Parnell feud. Some knowledgeable citizens put the number of men killed as high as 20, and for years after the gunfight, the participants and other family members and friends were extremely wary. Several left the state because of threats, and others took extreme precautions.

Dr. Hilton, who was involved on the Tucker side of the gunfight, would never enter a room without shades or blinds, and he refused to be seated where he couldn't see the door. It was truly a black mark in El Dorado's history and stories about the violence continues to this day.

***

In 1997, I traveled to Tombstone, Arizona, and watched the reenactment of the *Gunfight at the OK Corral*. If you haven't been to Tombstone, you probably won't just happen to pass through on your way to somewhere else. The town is off the main highway, and only Hollywood's glamorized history of the gunfight has kept the town from completely dying. Today tourism, based on the gunfight, has given the town a new life.

I came back from Tombstone with a lot of pictures, and an idea about the gunfight in El Dorado, which was as violent as the one in Tombstone. After convincing the El Dorado Advertising and Promotion Committee that it would be a good tourism draw, the reenactment was funded, and today, after being held each summer for the past 15 years, it is recognized a one of the premier events in the state, and one of the top 100 tour bus stops in the country.

However, as soon as it was made public that we were discussing a reenactment of the gunfight, I began to get visits and calls. The gist of the messages were to not to bring up any of El Dorado's dirty laundry: Specifically, the gunfight. Later, as I talked with others, it was not only the gunfight but as one old-timer told me, *"For God's sake, don't mention all that killing in the oil boom."*

As I researched and collected information about the gunfight, in preparation for a reenactment, I had a very distinguished, elderly gentleman stop by my office one day. He got right to the point: *"Richard, I think you should put aside any thoughts about the reenactment of that terrible gunfight. It is a black mark on this community that we have tried to put behind us. If you put on a reenactment of that horrible scene it will look bad for our city."*

Well, that conversation confirmed my thoughts about how difficult it is to obtain information about certain historical events. If those events are considered a black mark on the community, they are swept under the rug. My attempt to do a reenactment was, as the man stated to me…*"It would just be bad for the town. Don't do it."* I persisted and, today, the award-winning reenactment known as Showdown at Sunset has been produced by El Dorado's Main Street program for more than 15 years.

In a private conversation a few years back, former Gov. Tucker told me several interesting stories about the feud. He remembers his grandfather telling him about the gunfight, and how he lost an arm in an ambush in Union County; according to his grandfather, it was all the fault of the sorry Parnells.

As an almost comical side note, Gov. Tucker said his grandfather gave this account: *"I was lying on the ground seriously wounded, being tended to by Sheriff Norris, when my son held up the mail."*

"Look Daddy—I still have all the mail!"

According to Gov. Tucker, the older members of his family still held a grudge against the Parnells, and he was told that if he ever went to El Dorado he should be very careful because there were still hard feelings about the feud.

Gov. Tucker didn't think much about the stories his grandfather told him until he was a senior in high school. He was playing right defensive tackle for the Little Rock Central Tigers, and one of their games was in El Dorado's Memorial Stadium, the premier high school stadium in the state, built with oil money, naturally.

After the kickoff, he took the field and lined up, and right before the ball was snapped, he glanced across the line at the El Dorado offensive tackle. His eyes dropped down to the El Dorado tackle's jersey, and there stitched across his jersey was, *"Parnell."* Gov. Tucker recalls he never even heard the snap count as the big tackle looked at *"Tucker"* on his jersey, grinned, hit him, and sent him sprawling back.

"I got back up and let me tell you something: The rest of that game became a two-man battle, and the Parnells and the Tuckers were feuding again."

Gov. Tucker said his father had just returned to Little Rock after serving as a captain in World War II. El Dorado's football team was into town to play Little Rock Central. He attended the game that rainy day, and he was walking back from the game—in pouring rain—when a car full of girls, noting his army uniform, pulled up and offered him a ride. He gladly jumped in the car, and as they rode toward downtown Little Rock where he was staying, one of the girls asked him his name.

"I'm James Guy Tucker, from Little Rock," he said. Every eye was on him immediately, and the car pulled over.

"We're Parnells from El Dorado," one of the girls said. James Guy said they didn't say another word as he opened the car door and stepped back out in the rain.

8

BOOM!

IN El Dorado, the past should be noted as **B. B. or A. B.** That's **before the boom** and **after the boom.** The 1920s oil boom was, and will always be, the defining era in the history of the town. Although the little village had been shaken and deeply embarrassed by the Gunfight on the Square, the gunfight was just another incident, compared to what happened in and around the downtown during those first few years of the oil boom. A little, sleepy Southern village changed in the blink of an eye.

That change began at 4 p.m., Jan. 10, 1921, as a booming gusher blew in. It was on the edge of town, and the spray of oil that went through the wooden derrick kicked off a flood of fortune-seekers who supercharged this little village with oil money and new residents. It changed the little town of 3,800 rather-naive souls forever.

However, the boom did a lot more than increase the wealth and population of the community. Without a doubt, it did boost the town's prosperity and population, but those increases came with an extremely high price—a price measured by the thousands of murders, rapes, and robberies that plagued the community during the early 1920s.

A sleepy, southern village suddenly became a roaring, lawless oil boomtown, and it occurred in a startling short period of time. The community grew from 3,500 in January of 1921 to 50,000 or more in just 18 months. The influx of humanity that poured into

El Dorado was so great that only an estimate of the population was made.

After the huge Smackover Field was discovered in late 1922, so many newcomers arrived in South Arkansas that the small villages north of El Dorado, Norphlet and Smackover, with 500 to 700 in population, grew to more than 10,000 in weeks. The acres of tents that filled the fields around El Dorado held thousands more. And with these thousands of newcomers arrived the swindlers, hijackers, prostitutes, and other criminals.

Almost completely absent in this first flood of people were respectable women. However, women did come, thousands of them. They came from the brothels of north Louisiana and East Texas to El Dorado, the new boomtown place to be. In the early 1920s it was a time of complete chaos in South Arkansas, and many areas of the county were as lawless as the frontier towns of the Old West.

This influx of oil money, during the first five years of the oil boom, amounted to more than the appraised value of all the property in the state. However, the wealth of the oil boom didn't come without problems, and before the boom was finished, the community was shaken to its very foundation by the mayhem spawned by the boom.

Although the oil boom was just one of many historic events that affected the city over the past 150 years, it was by far the most significant. The oil boom of 1920s was a watershed that not only resulted in a proliferation of significant buildings, but it also changed and warped the mindset of the town.

Before the oil boom, the downtown consisted of mostly one- and two-story wooden frame buildings. As the oil boom money washed over the town, almost every structure in the downtown was leveled, and in their place came new multi-storied brick buildings and new churches. The old, redbrick, Victorian-style courthouse was razed and replaced with the biggest courthouse in the state, and, a few years later, a massive, concrete high school football stadium was built. Today, this stadium is still the biggest and most significant high school stadium in the state, and dwarfs most Division II college stadiums.

However, not only did the appearance of the El Dorado change, but this influx of money, along with the greed, violence, and general lawlessness it brought, changed and warped the character of the community. As the boom reached its peak, the open pastures west of town became tent cities with thousands of residents, and around this little, quaint downtown with its Victorian courthouse sprang tentacles of ramshackle development, particularly south of town toward the railroad station.

Down South Washington Avenue, bars, gambling houses, and whorehouses filled both sides of the street, and only an old cemetery was left without a building on it. During the early 1920s, at least 25 brothels also lined the dirt streets south of the courthouse square.

Before the boom, the streets were paved only around the courthouse, and dirt-and-gravel roads were the rule elsewhere in town. When it rains (and in South Arkansas, it rains frequently), those streets became quagmires as mules and oxen pulled heavy equipment offloaded from the railroad south of town to the oilfields north of town.

Because of the overwhelming impact of the oil boom, I have made the oil boom a centerpiece in the history of the community, and I have included several pages from a work of historical fiction to impart an understanding the nature of the boom, and how the boom affected the community.

And finally, as I collected the material to write this book, I came away convinced there is a definite link between the carnage that came with the boom, the early history of the community, and the paranormal events that are evident in the theater and downtown.

This is how it all began.

Several weeks before the discovery of oil in South Arkansas, Dr. Samuel Busey, who called himself a doctor and a geologist—although he was neither—took over a bankrupt drilling operation on the west edge of El Dorado—about a half-mile from the center of town. After spending several weeks raising money (actually selling stock in the drilling operation by going door to door in downtown El Dorado), Busey hired a new crew and began to deepen the well. According to local sources, he planned to drill deep enough to test a sandstone that had recently flowed natural gas southwest of El Dorado. If the well was a dry hole, as Busey was sure it would be, then he would solemnly tell his investors that the well—although it had indications of oil and gas—it was a dry hole.

"We were so close," he would tell them and then describe how they were just unlucky.

However, Busey wasn't unlucky at all, he was a seasoned oil promoter and his method of operation was to sell as much interest as he could in an open-ended trust, making sure he sold enough to have a handsome profit no matter what the outcome of the well.

An open-ended trust is illegal today, because for every share sold, it dilutes the value of the original shareholders. If the well happens to produce, the operator would declare a dividend and pay all the investors a percentage of the cash flow. Naturally, the original investors would ultimately receive a much lower percentage of the cash flow because of the addition of the new investors. However, many times the cash flow from some of the gushers, especially those in the Smackover Field, was so large that the checks received by the investors were enough to stifle any complaints about their dilution of interest.

If the well was a dry hole, then Busey would move to another town and repeat the process. After all, since there had never been a producing oil well in Arkansas, the odds that the # 1 Armstrong would be a dry hole were overwhelming. He was especially happy about taking over a suspended operation, because much of the cost had already been absorbed, and Busey would only have to drill another 500 feet, declare the well a dry hole, and move on. It had all the marking of a very profitable venture.

On Jan. 9, 1921, after a cold front had dumped rain on the location, followed by a strong north wind, the drilling reached to top of the sand Busey was seeking, and late that afternoon the crew set pipe, cemented it in the ground, and made ready to test the well. After the cement hardened, the bottom plug was drilled and the well was deepened another 10 feet into the sand, where the zone could be tested. After the bit reached that depth, the driller pulled the drill string out of the hole, and got ready to go into the hole with the swabbing cups.

In normal drilling operations, the hole is full of heavy mud that holds back any fluid or gas that may be in subsurface sand. In the 1920s, wells were allowed to blow in by removing the mud from the hole, which reduced the weight that held back the oil or gas. When the mud was removed from the hole and no oil or gas came to the surface, the operator would conclude the well was a dry hole.

By late that Sunday afternoon, "Dr." Busey was ready to test the well. According to statements from the drilling crew, the bailer had only pulled up five bailing runs when the well began to flow. At first the remaining mud came rushing out of the well-bore, and then with a mighty roar, as the pressure increased, the well began to spew oil.

In downtown El Dorado, less than a half-mile away, the plume of oil spraying up over the wooden derrick was a remarkable sight. When the townspeople realized what was happening, church bells began to ring, the sawmill whistle sounded, and the town emptied as the entire community rushed out of town to get an up-close view of the gusher.

That night there was a party that lasted until early the next morning and "Dr." Busey went on the radio announcing the well was capable of producing 30,000 barrels of oil a day and untold riches would be forthcoming to South Arkansas. Of course, the 30,000 barrels of oil was just a promoter's exaggeration, but the Busey Well, as it was called, did change South Arkansas and it did bring millions of dollars into the area.

The Busey well only produced for 54 days, producing an insignificant amount of oil, but it kicked off a drilling boom that resulted in almost 300 wells being drilling that year in South Arkansas. Of the 300 wells drilled, only 26 were dry holes and several of the producers were major discoveries.

The discovery of oil in South Arkansas changed a sleepy timber and farming town into a roaring, lawless boomtown—in just 18 months. I researched the boom and its many facets for several years before writing the novel The Queen of Hamburger Row, and I can tell you, that without a doubt, the first two years of the boom were unparalleled in the sordid life and instant wealth the boom produced.

The following excerpt is from my novel *The Queen of Hamburger Row*. It vividly describes the chaos that occurred during the oil boom. This is a dramatized account of the discovery.

CHAPTER ONE

"Oh, my God! No! Not more rain!" yelled Pete, trying to make himself heard over the noise of the motors. He backed off the brake and looked up at a darkening sky, where the first gust of wind announced another storm. He shook his head and spit a stream of tobacco juice out in the ditch beside the rig. Pete Dawson, the tool-pusher and driller on the drilling rig, and his crew had taken over the operations of the # 1 Armstrong in the middle of December after the original crew quit when the first operator ran out of money.

"Conroe, throw some more pine knots in the damn firebox. This rain's gonna cool the boiler off, and we ain't gonna have no power to run the rig," yelled Pete. Conroe, the youngest hand on the crew, had the worst job on the rig, doubling as a floor hand and a boiler fireman. He was responsible for keeping the steam boiler heated by having a roaring wood fire going at all times. Conroe plodded through the mud and he was almost to the firebox, when a clap of thunder and a flash of lightning stopped him, his hair stood on end, and a big pine tree on the edge of the field splintered...

"...By God, this job just can't get any worse, can it?" said Sam, the rail-thin derrick-man who constantly complained about being cold. "Y'all know when this cold front passes through, that north wind is gonna freeze our asses off, don't ya?"

Everyone associated with drilling this well had been eagerly anticipating something right below 1,900 feet where they had set casing, but nothing showed up. Now, the crew was holding their last two weeks' payroll checks until Hays could get fresh money transferred from Houston to the bank in South Arkansas. Hays Broadax, a money-raiser-promoter, was working with Dr. Samuel Busey, a doctor in name only, who had recently started calling himself a geologist. Dr. Busey, or Brother Busey to those whom Dr. Busey deemed to be religious, was a dignified, ramrod straight man who projected himself as a righteous doctor. Of course, he was too dignified to raise money. He never smiled but invoked an aura of seriousness that made the unwary susceptible to his soft and indirect approach, but beneath this facade was a promoter who had swindled hundreds of people across the country.

The roughnecks on the rig called Hays a "dandy," a "slicker." His voice and manner reminded one of smooth, soft silk, as an almost inextinguishable volume of words and phrases seemed to flood from his mouth containing the richest and most exaggerated phrases, yet with a sincerity; sometimes even a voice-trembling sincerity, that could put even the most conservative banker on the edge of their chair, hanging on every word as Hays enthralled them with tales of riches; wealth beyond their imagination, if only—if only, they would invest in the well Hays was promoting, and their cost, since they were friends of Hays, would be discounted so they were paying much, much less. Of course, everyone who invested was a special friend of Hays's.

***

"Y'all know this is just another dry hole, and we ain't gonna get a dime for workin' this past two weeks, don't ya?" said Sam. He spit a stream of tobacco juice out into the rain and turned back to the crew. "Hays is outta suckers. El Dorado ain't nothin' but a little hayseed town, and Hays done picked it clean. Them damned dirt farmers and loggers can't rub two nickels together."

"Yeah, I think we should just walk off this damn rig and give it to him," muttered Conroe, who might as well have been talking to the rig, since no one paid any attention to a green hand.

Pete, whose job was to keep the crew together, tried to settle them down.

"Now, come on, boys. All we got to do is swab this well a few times, and if nothing comes in, we'll be through. Y'all know Hays has always come through with the money. We'll get paid. Sam, go up on the floor, and check if anything looks promising from the first few swab runs.

Sam reluctantly pulled his slicker coat around him, bowed his head into the rain, and climbed up the slippery steps to the rig floor.

"Damn-it-to-hell, this sorry, job ain't worth it!" He wiped the water off his face and had to grab a handrail to keep from falling down on the slick floor. The crew had just pulled the fourth swab run without a sign of anything. He was just about to walk away, when he heard a bubbling, hissing sound coming from the casing.

"Damn, what was that?" He looked down at the mud that had started to bubble as it flowed out of the open pipe

"Yeah, by God! Yeah!" He took another whiff and yelled back down to Pete. "Pete, we's got something coming in!"

Hey! Somethin' bubblin'! Comin' from the pipe! Mud looks like it's gettin' cut!" he yelled.

"Go over and smell it. It might be gas!"

Sam bent down over the pipe so he could smell whatever was coming out of the pipe.

"Yeah, Pete! It's gas. There ain't no doubt about it; a damn good show! You need to come take a look. It's cuttin' the mud back a bunch!"

Pete walked out from under the tin shed into the rainstorm just as a bolt of lightning hit another tree beside the rig.

"Oh, my God!" screamed Pete.

The blinding flash sent everybody to the ground for a few seconds. Pete pulled himself out of the mud and headed on up to the rig floor as the rainstorm swirled around him.

"Damn, Pete! I wouldn't get on that rig floor right now! The next one might hit the derrick!" yelled Conroe.

Pete ignored him and continued to climb the steps up to the rig floor. He could feel his pulse quicken at the thought that they might be in an oil sand. Gas always beat oil up the hole, and unless it was just a small pocket of lignite gas, they could be onto something…

"…Oh, my God!" Pete yelled to Sam. "This damn thing could be dry gas! Might blow us off the rig! They was five men killed south of here when that Constantine well kicked! Get ready to run, if I tell you! Hey! Wait a minute! I hears somethin' else!"

Pete yelled and turned toward Sam, "Get off the floor, Sam! She's comin' in!" Pete scrambled for the steps just as a spray of gas-cut mud kicked out of the casing, drenching both of them.

"What the hell?" questioned Sam, who had been on a number of wells, but had never seen one come in.

"Damn it, Sam! Get your ass off the floor! Or you're gonna have it blown off!" screamed Pete. He scurried down the ladder and headed for the shed as the gas and mud flow picked up to a roar, and a few speckles of oil began to froth up from the mud, sending a spray of oil over the rig floor. Then, as Pete and Sam hit the ground and ran for the shed, the casing rattled, an earsplitting roar of gas and mud spewed out of the open pipe, and a few seconds later a solid stream of crude oil shot 10 feet in the air followed by another slug of oil which reached halfway up the derrick ... Suddenly, there was an earsplitting roar as the rig shook and the full column of oil reached the top of the derrick.

Conroe yelled, "Oh, my God! Run! Run!" He had never seen anything like this in his life, and he broke and ran, splashing out across the open field through the rainstorm and oil spray until he was at least a hundred yards away.

"Just stand back, boys! Let her blow!" yelled Pete, trying to be heard over the roar. "Hays done told me if the well was to come in, not to shut it in. Hell, I think he wants to bring some of his investors out to show 'em. Hey, maybe we'll get paid now. Donald, go get Conroe and tell him this thing ain't dangerous, but by God, don't nobody light up a smoke, or you'll be a fried chicken in about ten seconds. Sam, take the truck into town and go to the Arcade Hotel. See if you can find Hays. Tell him we got a well blowing in! Get Dr. Busey and his people out here as soon as he can!"

"Pete, there ain't no way that damn old truck can make it outta this mudhole," said Sam as he surveyed the deep mud surrounding the rig.

"Well, it ain't but a half-mile, so get your ass walkin' and hurry. This damn well might bridge over and kill itself. Hays needs to get his people out here as quick as he can. Get goin'!"

Early that Friday morning, as the rain let up and people started getting out, Sam walked into the downtown square.

"The well has done come in! Oil's everywhere! We done hit a gusher!" he yelled at the top of his lungs as he pointed west to where a cloud of oil spewed from the wooden derrick.

Soon Sam had a crowd of people around him, and in a few minutes people were running, shouting the news, and a stream of cars roared out of town heading for the drilling rig. Church bells began to ring and the steam whistle at the Loutre Brothers sawmill sounded as virtually everyone in town rushed to the downtown square or headed for the rig.

Later that day Pete turned the well into a large earthen pit that they had dug, where the oil could be held until it was picked up by a tanker truck and hauled to a refinery. Dr. Busey held a press conference in the lobby of the Arcade Hotel that afternoon.

"First, let me thank everyone for coming," he said as he surveyed a room packed with people and reporters.

"As you know, this huge oil well that I have just brought in is making thousands of barrels of oil a day."

"Dr. Busey?" A reporter for The Shreveport Times who had driven up from Louisiana had a question. "How many barrels would you estimate the well is making?"

"Thirty thousand barrels a day!" Dr. Busey said raising his finger in an exclamation point.

"Thirty thousand?" the reporter gasped.

"Yes, and that's a conservative estimate," Dr. Busey went on to say.

Before Dr. Busey had even finished the news conference, reporters were running for the phones, and when the papers hit the newsstands the next day, the headlines, "30,000 Barrels a Day!" were splashed across the front pages of newspapers across the Mid-South in 2-inch-high letters.

The citizens of El Dorado celebrated all afternoon and well into the night.

The day after the well came in, folks in El Dorado heard a continuous steam whistle from a special train approaching the Rock Island Station. There were two white flags flying from the front of the engine, which was pulling five passenger coaches. It was the first of hundreds of special trains that would arrive in El Dorado over the next few months. The third day after the strike, five special trains arrived from Little Rock, and within six months more than 20 trains a day were coming in and out of the Rock Island or the Missouri Pacific station.

When this deluge of humanity flooded into town, El Dorado had few if any prostitutes. At first, the few girls who were plying their trade asked and received astronomical prices for their services, but when the tales of these high-priced prostitutes reached places like Galveston and other wide-open towns in Texas and Louisiana, a flood of prostitutes invaded the city. Barrelhouses, the saloons where gambling and prostitution flourished and whiskey was served, were thrown up by the dozens. Several barrelhouses even sent their prostitutes out to the oilfields on horseback to service their customers because nothing was off limits.

Before the first year of the boom was over, this mass of humanity had strained the fabric of the community, and the few law officers in town had given up trying to control the thousands of thieves who preyed on the oil boom masses. The city of El Dorado would survive this onslaught of lawlessness, but hundreds of these newcomers wouldn't.

The townspeople had been infected with a deadly virus and its symptoms were evident. Greed drove them to steal, covet, take, and ignore the human misery. Nothing interfered with the accumulation of wealth, and city leaders rented their buildings at astronomical prices. If it was for a barrelhouse, they made sure the lease was in a maid's name. They lived a charade as they ignored the hundreds of murders, and treated the mayhem, gambling, and prostitution, as if it were happening in another state.

The local newspaper ignored the violence, regulating it to small clips on the back page, and the polite parlor talk never mentioned it. During the early 1920s El Dorado was a town sinking into the slime of Hamburger Row."

Taken from the novel, *The Queen of Hamburger Row.*

9

HAMBURGER ROW —LIFE IN A CESSPOOL

TODAY, if you drive down Washington Avenue past the Union County Courthouse, and continue south toward Hillsboro Street, you'll find it hard to imagine what the street looked like during the early years of the oil boom.

In the 1920s, paved streets ended a block from the square just south of the Garrett Hotel, where today BanCorpSouth is located. As the street dropped down toward the railroad station, a mixture of dirt and gravel served as the roadbed. The street was lined with wooden, ramshackle, one and two-story, unpainted buildings. These were fronted with wooden sidewalks, where young boys sold moonshine in Coke bottles for $1.25, prostitutes beckoned you in, and dope dealers pulled at your sleeve.

The railroad station, about a quarter mile down the street, was adjacent to a muddy lot called Muleskinner's Corner where loads of heavy equipment were placed on wagons pulled by teams of oxen or mules. Some of the teams consisted of as many as 20 oxen, and the iron-rimmed wagons loaded with oilfield equipment dug deep into South Washington Avenue as the wagons headed north toward the oilfields. When the spring rains flooded South Arkansas, the street became a quagmire where mules and oxen actually drowned in the street.

To give you a better feeling of the unbelievable conditions along Hamburger Row during the early 1920s, I have inserted a bit more of my novel, which describes in detail the squalor and depravity.

The Queen of Hamburger Row

In 1921, if there had been a hell on earth, surely Hamburger Row would have been a leading candidate for the dishonor, as it seethed in the mid-summer heat spewing stench from open sewers along with the putrid reek of dead mules that had drowned in the deeper mud holes, still buried in the mucky, filthy street, mingled with the aroma of cheap perfume worn by the prostitutes, who paraded up and down the sidewalks, pulling at the sleeves of any man who looked half-way prosperous.

The depravity of the street wouldn't have been complete without the dope peddlers like Smiling Jack or Weasel, who offered you something to make you "feel good" as they grabbed your elbow, or the petty pickpockets, other assorted thieves, and drunks, the refuse of a nation, who tried to steal anything of value. They all contributed to make El Dorado's Hamburger Row hell on earth.

The water from recent rains simmered in the wallowed-out muddy street and a haze of steam and stench permeated the entire area during the day, as the putrid smell of sewage, dead mules, perfumed whores, and smoke from the open fires boiled up from the bowels of Hamburger Row spewing out, what seemed to be a caustic gas from the nadir of hell, challenging all who would enter the depths of this depravity to beware; danger lurked…

She stopped outside and looked up at the building, and the sight of Jake's Place. Its massive, two-story front, which dominated the buildings around it was enough to stop most people who stood and wondered how such an enormous monstrosity could exist. The building had been thrown up quickly, and sloppy construction made for an uneven floor that was always soiled with sawdust, tobacco juice, and spilt beer. The bar was made of massive logs nailed together and covered with a plank front, and the seats at the bar were crosscut log sections on which the whores perched like birds begging for favors...

The girls were back inside when Masha walked up to Jake's Place, and she hesitated, but finally got up the courage to push open one of the red doors and step into the saloon. To her, a step inside Jake's Place was like stepping into a smelly cesspool, as a thick, moisture-laden cloud of tobacco smoke, cheap perfume, and spilt beer hung in the air, startling her senses. She looked around and noticed men standing at the bar with girls who were touching, rubbing, and begging for attention: "Buy me a drink—-Lookin' for a little fun?" they mumbled as they solicited every man that stepped inside.

Masha was appalled and bewildered at the crowd of yelling and cursing men, scantily clothed girls, and husky bouncers, and she was on the verge of panic and was about to step back outside when one of the girls spotted her and walked over.

"Hi, I'm Masha Carrington from Locust Bayou," she said to the snow-white blonde who was looking at Masha shaking her head.

"Well, hello, Miss Masha, I'm Darlene from Waco. What in the hell are you doin' here at Jake's Place?" Darlene was a broken-down, pitiful specter of a once-beautiful woman whose malnourished body, gaunt from the lack of nourishing food, seemed to reflect a species of some bird. She resembled a crane-like, stilted person on thin legs—the flesh clinging to her bones.

It took Masha a few seconds to collect her thoughts. Then she said, "I thought maybe you could help me find a place to stay. Uh, well, I had some problems at home, and I had to leave. I've looked all over town and there doesn't seem to be a room to rent."

"Girl, this here town is full to the brim, and they ain't a place nowheres, especially for women, but let me let you talk with Sylvia, she's kinda in charge of the girls that stay here."

"Do y'all work here?"

"Well, I guess you could call it work, 'cause it shor pays real well."

"What?"

Darlene pulled Masha up close to her and whispered.

"Damn, Masha, don't you know what we do?"

"No."

"Girl, we sells, or I might say, rents ourselves to a gentleman for a short period of time," Darlene said as she winked at Masha.

Masha gasped as she realized what the girls were selling. She had thought they were just greeters and entertainers who came out front to get men to come into the saloon. Oh my God! Oh my God; I'm in a whorehouse!

"Want a job, honey?"

End of *The Queen of Hamburger Row*

10

THE OLD 1921, RIALTO THEATER

ALONG with the oil boom and thousands of newcomers came the desire for entertainment, and the girls in the barrelhouses weren't enough to satisfy the demand. That desire spawned the building of new El Dorado movie theaters, or picture shows as they were called. After a few years, El Dorado boasted 10 theaters of various sizes, located mostly in the downtown area. However, the Rialto Theater was always the dominant theater in the city, even from its early days.

The current Rialto Theater, as its marquee says, is *"The Last of Arkansas' Grand Theaters."* However, it may surprise you that this 80-year-old theater is the 'new' Rialto, rebuilt on the shell of the original 1921 theater. The old theater, and, of course, the new Rialto, has an extremely colorful history, and that history begins immediately after the construction of the first Rialto Theater.

The old 1921–1925 Rialto was a low-ceilinged, one-story building featuring a makeshift front on which vaudeville shows were advertised, as well as large sandwich billboard that sat out beside the building. There were basement dressing rooms for the live performances and cut-glass chandeliers hung in the auditorium and foyer. Evidently, from all accounts, the theater enjoyed a relatively quiet beginning and nothing of relative interest occurred until Jan. 10, 1921, at 4 p. m. It was just as the early theater workers were coming in to set up the reels for the 5 o'clock picture show, when they heard a hissing and then a roar coming from west of the theater. The theater workers and most of the citizens of the town, rushed out in the street to look west where a wooden oil derrick was standing. A monster gusher of oil was cascading skyward through the top of the derrick. It marked the start of the South Arkansas oil boom.

Business owners who were already operating in El Dorado were ecstatic about all the new customers who were arriving daily, and the Rialto began to schedule shows starting as early as 9 in the morning, continuing on until midnight.

Along with the influx of oil workers and promoters, came the nation's riffraff who were like rats drawn to cheese, following easy money from boomtown to boomtown. Drug dealers, prostitutes, and criminals flocked to El Dorado, and the leaders of these gangs of hoodlums bought land on South Washington Street across from the railroad station and began to build barrelhouses.

Barrelhouses, which were saloons with gambling and prostitution, were openly advertised, and in 1921 and 22 they sprouted like weeds in a new garden. Young boys sold moonshine for $1.25 a Coke bottle on the street corners, and prostitutes stood out in front of the barrelhouses urging the crowds of men that filled the street to come in for some fun. However, the carnival-like atmosphere disappeared as night fell on the area south of the courthouse square, and following the blackness, (no street lights) came the most notorious and dangerous of the newcomers:

The oilmen called them hijackers. These gangs of killers roamed the back alleyways of South Washington Avenue. By mid-1921, South Washington Avenue had picked up the name Hamburger Row, from the open grills that filled the sidewalks. In the dark alleyways along Hamburger Row and Cedar Street, these gangs of murders would assault almost anyone foolish enough to walk along the dark sidewalks alone. The hijackers were robbers, whose method of operation was to hit a man with a lead-weighted club, knife him, and then strip him of anything valuable. A mortuary wagon came by early every morning to collect sometimes as many as a dozen bodies.

But despite the squalor and dangerous conditions, the throngs of opportunists still came. In less than two years, the population grew to an estimated 50,000, and the few law enforcement officers in the city and county gave up on enforcing the law south of Main Street.

The Rialto was right in the middle of this mass of humanity, and tales began to circulate about happenings in the theater, especially during the last midnight show. Prostitutes began to frequent the theater and the center of the back row—away from the sidewall lighting—was called "Whores' row."

When the oil boom and thousands of boom followers hit El Dorado like a whirlwind, several enterprising individuals showed up eager to take advantage of these entertainment-starved customers, and late in the fall of 1920 ground was broken for a new theater—The Rialto. Even though the construction was hurried and the workers lacked the bricklaying and building skills, in the summer of 1921 the 400-seat theater opened for business to a packed crowd—a packed crowd for every "picture show." Shows started early in the morning and continued until midnight.

The construction was indeed hurried, but theater owners did take time to build a large vaudeville stage, basement dressing rooms, and a sunken orchestra pit that would hold 15 musicians. The following comments are from a member of a 12-piece orchestra that played for silent movies and vaudeville shows in the old original theater. (As soon as the theater opened, vaudeville shows played every weekend and silent movies filled the screen when a live show wasn't available. Each silent movie and even the early "talkies" came with reams of sheet music for the orchestra.)

Ms. Alta Jensen of Smackover, who was 92 at the time she gave this interview in 1990, remembers those early movies in the

1920s—movies such as *Birth of a Nation* and *The Hunchback of Notre Dame*, especially the musical scores.

She played bass violin in a 12-piece orchestra in the old Rialto Theater from 1922 to 1927, under the direction of her husband and conductor, Oliver Jensen. She and fellow musicians brought life to the silent movies and vaudeville touring shows.

Ms. Jensen, a native of Indianapolis, Indiana, learned music from her future husband as a teen-ager. After he served in World War I, the couple was married on Nov. 6, 1920.

"We worked together for about 52 years. We came to El Dorado because of the oil boom. It was terrible. We couldn't find a place to live."

Living space was so scarce when the Jensens arrived in 1921, they couldn't find lodging, so they joined a traveling road show and came back to El Dorado a year later.

"We went on the road with a show and came back in 1922. The town wasn't a safe place," she said.

When Mr. and Mrs. Jensen settled in El Dorado, their first accommodations were cots rented for 50-cents in someone's yard. They later moved to an apartment that was nothing more than a shack.

"It was just a chicken house. We had one burner to cook on, two plates, and two cups."

Mrs. Jensen said she was afraid a lot of the time because of violence on the street.

"There was always somebody shooting guns. They had to shoot to warn about fires and there were fires all the time. (During the first few years of the oil boom, numerous downtown buildings burned including the Armstrong Building on the square.) *A lot of oil burned, and a lot of those wooden buildings burned. We never knew what was going on, whether it was people shooting at each other or warning about a fire."*

Musicians at the Rialto Theater worked until about midnight. After playing their instruments for four hours, with a 15-minute break between two-hour shows, the group would walk home.

"We had to walk down the middle of the (Cedar) street to avoid being hit. If we walked on the sidewalk next to the buildings we could have been hurt by objects or people being thrown out the windows." (Note: Pedestrians walking from the Rialto on Cedar Street would pass by Mrs. Smith's hotel on the corner of Washington Avenue and Cedar Street. The hotel was noted for its rowdy guests, who were mainly oilfield roughnecks.)

Sometimes even the middle of the street was not a good place to walk: Mrs. Jensen recalls a mule drowning in a mudhole in a city street.

"The streets were so muddy and oily. The heavy oxen and wagons with steel wheels carrying equipment cut deep into the ground. A mule sank down into the mud and couldn't get out."

Because the orchestra played continuously during the movies, Mrs. Jensen was able to collect a large amount of sheet music over the years.

"We played a lot of shows. Some of them had one hundred pieces of music. I donated a truckload of music to one college."

Mrs. Jensen's comments about how dangerous it was to walk the streets, especially after dark, have led some to speculate that the rumored tunnel from the basement of the Rialto to the basement of the Union County Courthouse a block away was constructed during this time period. It seems that because of the danger involved, being able to bypass the alleyways off South Washington Avenue and Jefferson Avenue where hijackers lurked made the tunnel seem necessary.

If there is or was a tunnel to the courthouse from the Rialto it would have been around 300 feet long. While 300 feet doesn't seem like a great distance, the two areas it connected were as different as daylight and dark. In 1921 and 22, one block south of the courthouse was like a step back in time to the lawless Old West where law enforcement was non-existent. As Mrs. Jensen commented, they were afraid to walk down the sidewalk and even in the middle of the street because of the danger. On the other hand, the small El Dorado police force and sheriff's office was in the courthouse, and the area around the courthouse square was regularly patrolled.

In my opinion the tunnel—if there was one—was built for safety reasons, and when the danger of walking the streets near the theater declined, or when a tragic accident was rumored to have occurred in the tunnel, the entrances were bricked up, and under the prevailing cloak of "don't talk, don't tell" it was all brushed into the dustbin of history. (I'll cover more of the rumors concerning the tunnel in a later chapter.)

The oil boom, which caused the population of the city to soar to more than 50,000, also caused a boom in movie theaters or picture shows as they were called in the 1920s. The newspaper article below is an overview of the theater expansion due to the oil boom. The information will give you a better understanding of how adding nearly 50,000 people to the population of a city can increase the entertainment business.

Movie Theater History—El Dorado, Arkansas (from an Oct. 28, 1971, *El Dorado Daily News* story)

In 1917 E. C. Robertson, a Texan, moved to El Dorado and opened El Dorado's first movie theater, the Mission Theater at 109 East Main Street. In the spring of 1921 the McWilliams family opened the Rialto Theater, and in the fall of 1925 the company remodeled the Rialto Theater, even though it had been constructed only four years before. Workers installed more modern equipment, and total costs of the improvements rose to some $20,000.

In 1928 the old theater was demolished and the present theater was constructed on the site of the old Rialto. (Author's note: Based on old photographs, the east wall, the basement, and the orchestra pit of the old theater were incorporated into the new theater.) With the last principles tending towards acoustical perfection embodied in its construction, the new $250,000 Rialto Theater opened as one of the most modern sound-perfect playhouses in the Southwest. W. B. Smith was the contractor of the new building.

The new building seated 1400 people in its main floor and two balconies. The first floor held some nine hundred while the balconies held some five hundred occupants.

Velour draperies were used throughout the theater to deaden any sound that would tend to distort the presentation of talking pictures. Underlying the draperies covering each large wall is a layer of Azite, a padding which is said to prevent reverberation of sound. The walls are hung with draperies and the screen set is surrounded by folds of velour.

The stage thirty-two feet deep and sixty feet wide was ample room for the presentation of larger road shows. A $12,000 Mohler pipe organ was installed and short organ presentations were often presented. (Note: the organ and all the pipes are still in the theater.)

A washed air ventilating system was used to cool the theater which at the time was the latest thing out and the price of such a luxury was $6500. The heating system of the building was located in the basement of the building that also included dressing rooms and the theater separate power transformer and switchboard. The transformer was provided to insure a steady supply of current when the electric power was off on the regular line.

Two large electric signs were installed at the front and side of the building using 15,000 light bulbs.

The latest in talking picture equipment, two large projection machines using Western Electric systems were used upon opening. The machines would handle both Movietone and Vitaphone films and were valued at a cost of $15,000.

Kolben, Hunter and Boyd were the architects for the building and King Studios of Dallas supervised the hanging of the draperies and other acoustical features of the new theater.

The very first movie shown at the Rialto was "Street Girl", a musical drama that was declared an outstanding hit of the season at that time. The film presented Betty Compson and her violin in a delightful story of a street waif who wins her way to fame as a member of a small band of musicians.

Some other famed films showing after the grand opening were "The Cock-Eyed World", "Frozen Justice", "The Coconuts", "Hit The Deck", "No, No Nannette", "The Vagabond Lover", "On With The Show", and many, many more famous shows of that time.

It was noted that in 1939, "Gone With The Wind" had a premier showing. This theater was the first to show this picture in this part of Arkansas, Louisiana, and Texas. It played for an unprecedented 19 days at the extravagant price of one dollar.

Between the time of construction of the old Rialto in 1921 and 1924 there were 7 additional theaters opened in downtown El Dorado. In the 1924 Pages City Directory nine theaters are listed. They were the Dillingham Theater, 213 East Cedar Street, the Fairview Theater, 545 East E and B street, the Majestic Theater, 212 South Washington Street, the Manhattan Theater, 210 North Washington Avenue, the Mission Theater, 109 East Main street, the Rex Theater, 418 South Washington Avenue, the Rialto Theater, 111 East Cedar, the St. Louis theater, 424 North West Avenue and the Star theater, 123 West Hillsboro street.

By 1927 several theaters closed, but a number of new theaters opened to give downtown El Dorado an all time high of 10 theaters. The new theaters were Arkansas Amusement, 116 Petroleum Building, the Plaza theater, 231 Liberty street and the Princess theater, 209 North Jefferson street. In the 1949 Polk's City Directory the list had shrunk to 5 theaters with additions that included the Ritz Theater at 217 East Main and the Savoy Theater, 624 North West Avenue.

11

THE NEW RIALTO

IN 1920, after the discovery of oil in south Arkansas, the population of El Dorado surged, and the original 1921 Rialto Theater immediately became too small to handle the influx of customers.

In 1925, the 4-year-old Rialto was remodeled and expanded at a cost of $20,000, but it soon became obvious that a much larger theater was needed. In 1928, with oil money flooding the city and the old remodeled 1925 Rialto packed every night and day, a group of businessmen made a commitment to build a new theater. In the spring of 1928, the plans were ready for a new, much larger theater, which would seat 1,400. It was budgeted to cost a staggering $250,000 in 1929 dollars, which would easily translate into several million today.

Of course, the first of the numerous stories concerning the new theater revolve around the torrid construction of the "new" Rialto. Supposedly, in order to keep customers during construction, they hired a firm that promised a quick job, with men even working at night. These workers were recruited from the hoards of men who came for the oil boom, desperately needing work. And even though they had little experience in bricklaying and working with steel beams at heights of over 70-feet off the ground, they started the construction work in the summer of 1928 after tearing down the old Rialto to a shell, leaving only the outer walls, orchestra pit, and basement.

As soon as the steelwork of the theater began taking shape, stories about accidents started to drift out and rumors about unskilled construction workers killed while working on the roof beams became widespread around town. It is very likely the foreman for the construction site spent part of his day up and down Hamburger Row offering jobs to an assortment of men, most of whom didn't have a clue about working on a huge building with overhead steel, such as the Rialto.

The demolition of the old Rialto had gone quick enough, but after some sighting of mysterious mists and noises coming from the remaining, original basement section (where the vaudeville dressing room had been), some of the construction crew refused to work on the night shift. However, more workers were recruited, and the steel work started up on time. When the building peaked out, the upper steelwork was over 70-feet above street level.

One of the rumors about accidents during construction has been passed around for several generations. Saturday night, after a mid-afternoon downpour, a construction crane was lifting the final beams of steel that would form the roof framework. The wind whipped the beam around and a tragic accident occurred. A steelworker from Brooklyn, who had worked on New York skyscrapers before coming to South Arkansas to get rich in the oil boom, was the crew leader. Evidently, workers ignored the windy and wet conditions, and beam after beam rose from the ground.

This description of the rumored accident is merely a guess about how it happened:

He shook his head as he watched the beams sway from side to side in the wind. Then, just as the final roof beam reached the top of the building, where the steel crew waited with bolts to fasten it to the frame of the building, a strange thing happened. According to one worker, just as the beam passed the last level of the building and someone reached to pull it to him, a cold mist seem to rise from the beam. There was a startled yell from the worker, and then as the rest of the crew watched in horror. A gust of wind sent the beam straight toward the startled worker, knocking him from the perch, and he fell off the building screaming as he fell into the structure's interior. Then as the crew drew back and watched, the mist remained for an entire minute, even with the wind gusting up to 20 mph.

The scream and the sight of the falling worker attracted the attention of the job foreman, who rushed to the back of the framed-up theater to find the worker dead on the concrete floor.

The following is a guess at what the ensuing conversation might have been: *"Hell, I ain't got no idea what his name is. He's just a bum we hired down on Hamburger Row,"* the foreman probably said. There was a moment of silence as he looked at the body, thinking of the delays and a possible investigation and other legal problems that were sure to surface if the municipal authorities were called. *"Put 'em down front where that next cement pour is going to be made."*

The crew nodded, knowing the bum from Hamburger Row wouldn't be missed, and the municipal authorities would ignore his death. Soon the shallow grave was dug and covered, and, before the morning shift started, cement was poured over the grave. It may be that the crew working that night were given a bonus, and told not to mention the accident. However, they did talk about it and the reason for the fall, and as the building topped out and interior work started there were rumors of strange sounds coming from the back of the theater. Many were of the opinion that the buried worker was haunting the theater.

In the barrelhouses along Hamburger Row, men would talk about this strange accident and the stories about the mist and the sudden swing of the beam would come into the conversation; again and again they would point to there being something supernatural about the accident.

In 1929, the crews who worked on the interior of the building doing high plasterwork on the beams, reported accident after accident which made the job one of the most dangerous in town. Of course, the job foreman maintained publicly that the crews were untrained and the minor accidents were the fault of men not understanding their job. However, privately, others expressed their concern that something supernatural was behind problems on the job, and many of the construction workers swore they would be glad when the job was over.

Of course, since much of the construction crew was paid in cash, trying to document the various crews that worked on the theater is almost impossible. However, according to other rumors, the tunnel that connected the old Rialto basement to the basement of the redbrick, Victorian courthouse was repaired; and as the basement work continued, work crews were brought in to repair and enlarge the tunnel. (Note: the above comments about the theater construction are based on the flimsiest of rumors, and although there is a strong possibility that serious accidents occurred during construction of the theater, there is no direct evidence.)

As soon as the new Rialto opened, it became the preeminent, glamour movie theater of the Mid-South, with white-gloved ushers and the finest in heating and cooling. Its acoustics were the best available, and it hosted regional premieres of such films as Gone With The Wind.

However, years passed and the theater slowly drifted into disrepair until finally, in the late 1970s, the single-screen theater closed; a victim of multi-screen mall theater competition. Then, in 1987, the theater regained a new lease on life when the balcony was divided into two theaters and, for a time, the Rialto came back with hits like Jurassic Park and Titanic. The theater operated for another 20 years as a triple-screen, first-run movie house, until the late fall of 2007 when it closed again.

However, the theater didn't stay closed long. In 2009, after an extensive renovation, the Rialto Theater reopened as a live music venue. The old concession stand and lobby were changed into Marylyn's at the Rialto, featuring an adult setting with drinks and live entertainment. Recently, the theater sold to El Dorado Festivals and Events, LLC. The Rialto Theater will be the centerpiece of a $50-million entertainment complex that will be operational by 2015.

***

The theater and the blocks around the building have a wealth paranormal history beginning with the Rialto's earliest days. These stories of supernatural occurrences, legends, and rumors have abounded, including just about everything—from construction workers killed while building the theater, to prostitutes being knifed in the balcony or thrown off the roof. And, of course, according to local legend, their ghosts and many more still roam the theater and the area around it.

In the chapters ahead, I will delve into more of those numerous paranormal events and tragic misdeeds associated with the Rialto Theater and the blocks around it.

12

A TOUR OF THE NEW (1929) RIALTO [BEFORE IT RE-OPENED IN 2009]

I have owned the Rialto Theater for more than 25 years, and during that time, I have nosed around and explored every corner of the old building. The more I have gotten to know the old theater, the more fascinated I've become, and not only about the building itself, but the history and paranormal occurrences associated with it, and, of course, the immediate blocks adjacent to the theater.

Before we delve into the details of some of the more intriguing paranormal occurrences that have been witnessed in the theater and its environs, let me take you on a tour of the old building as it stands today. After sitting empty for three years following its closure in 1984, the old building developed a very interesting aura, and few people could enter the building without feeling something strange and unusual as they walked through it.

Imagine an ancient theater, sadly drooping from neglect, with cobwebs stretching across its doors and an occasional roach scampering across the faded carpet. There is a musty smell in the air, faintly hinting of perfume—and a lingering, moldy smell of dampness hangs like a scepter over the cracked, plaster ceiling and walls. Light fixtures flicker as the current seems to waver, and occasionally the sound of wood groaning and feet walking on hidden steps breaks the silence.

Somewhere in the inner recesses of the theater, there are clicks on the tile floor from a woman wearing high heels as she walks into the restroom up on the mezzanine level, but the sound fades—no one is there. And as you enter the dimly lit lobby with its high—20-foot—plastered ceiling and Art Deco light fixtures, sometimes a whiff of perfume may greet you. But of course, there's no one around with any perfume on. And other times the lights on the statue of the Lady of the Rialto will fade as if someone has them on a dimmer. But no—the lights aren't on a dimmer. The wiring is new and all the bulbs have been changed several times.

A step into the vaulted, spacious main auditorium is enough to make a first-time visitor gasp. The 60-foot ceilings and the art deco presidium cast off an eerie glow in the dim light, and for just a minute your mind might wander back to a time when white-gloved ushers escorted dignified theater attendees to their seats. As you stroll down the aisle to the orchestra pit, you might still hear the 12-piece orchestra that played for silent movies. But then, you notice something unusual about the orchestra pit, and upon closer examination, you marvel at the 1908 Mahler pipe organ still sitting exactly where is was installed some 90 years ago. Above and beside the main stage are two, large slotted recesses that hold a bevy of organ pipes, waiting for a signal—an impulse—a blast of air from a blower in the basement that will send a whistle of sound from their lips reminiscent of *The Phantom of the Opera.*

Now, let's return to the outside of the theater, and enter as the African Americans (then called "colored") patrons of another era would have entered—not from the front main entrance, but from a side door on Jefferson Avenue. A few steps into the small foyer for these patrons, and you are in front of the hidden ticket booth.

Your ticket price is the same as the "whites only" ticket, but you don't get to sit in the spacious main auditorium and be ushered in by white-gloved usherettes. No, you don't even get to sit in the front section of the balcony. An arrow points to a narrow, dark doorway and a set of 66 stairs. A dim, bare light bulb hangs from a landing on the stairs, partially lighting the way to the back of the upper balcony, where a solid 3-foot wall separates the balcony "colored" from the "white" patrons. The old stairwell seems to vanish behind a low wall that blocks the "white" patron's view.

The old, original projection booth partially divides the balcony into two sections. The inside plaster walls of the old projection booth are covered with graffiti, as well as carved, sometimes dated, initials put there by the hundreds of projectionists and their friends who manned and visited the booth during the theater's early days. This large projection booth is the dominant feature of the upper balcony. It was where the spotlights for vaudeville performers were kept, as well as projection equipment for silent "picture shows" and then—as "talkies" came along—for the sound and projection equipment.

In the upper section of the balcony, located on the northwest corner of the theater, is a sliding, serving window where concessions were sold to "colored" patrons. Its well-worn, wooden shelves indicate years of use. Within this old concession area are two other items of interest.

As you enter through the small door to where theater employees sold popcorn and Cokes, there is a decrepit wooden ladder extending upward to a hole in the ceiling. Further examination reveals that this ladder allows access to the Rialto's attic of the theater—a 4-to-6-foot-high crawl or creep space extending over the entire theater. The roof-supporting beams and rafters make a lacework of perilous footing because between the 3-foot, spaced rafters there is only a thin layer of acoustic tile.

When the theater was in operation, the theater's maintenance crew used the crawl space in the attic to repair and replace bulbs in the ceiling light fixtures of the main auditorium. This unlit attic is a dangerous place because workers have to stay on the main rafters; one false step or slip could send someone plunging through the thin acoustical tile and then 60 feet to their death.

There is a sad, rumored story of a young man, eager to please, who was on his first job in the theater, rushing to scramble to the far south end of the theater to the main screen to change out several bulbs. Suddenly, there was a scream, *"Oh! Help!"* and then *"Ahaaaaaaa!"* echoed through the theater as he tumbled 60 feet from the attic and landed sprawled across the rail to the orchestra pit. Is this young man's spirit one of the ghosts who make themselves known in the orchestra pit area? Maybe.

As we take a closer look at the ladder to the attic, we see a 3-foot cap that leads to the roof. A good shove sends the cap tumbling onto the huge flat roof, and if you climb up the ladder another few feet, you can step out on the roof of the theater. It's an expanse of some 5,000 square feet of open rooftop. One of the projectionists who manned the upstairs booth for decades told stories about numerous workers who climbed the ladder, sometimes bringing with them moonshine, to party on the roof while the movie was playing. And, of course, where moonshine, men, and women are, there are also mixed tales of love, lust, fights, and, yes, rumored murders—all stemming from the roof of the theater.

There is one recurring, rumored tale of two women who loved the same man. They found each other on the roof and a violent fight ensued. According to one observer, the fight continued until one of the women ran to the south end of the roof, chased by the other; and when the first woman reached the 3-foot parapet wall, she was pushed over, falling nearly 70 feet to her death in an alley behind the theater.

Now let's return to the lobby and enter the main auditorium through one of the six doors. When you enter this magnificent auditorium—with its 60-foot-high walls, massive fluted organ encasements, and full stage—there's sometimes a feeling that the air is heavy. A weight seems to accompany the rush of cool air from the interior no matter how hot or humid it is outside the theater. Shadows seem to flicker from the faux box seats above the auditorium, and in the orchestra pit, where a 12-piece orchestra once played for silent films, the old original Mahler Pipe organ will occasionally make a deep monotone hum.

As you walk down the long aisle toward the left side of the stage, an open door awaits those who dare venture down the narrow stairwell into the basement where other mysteries await. A rickety set of six steps leads you to an open hallway flanked by the old vaudeville dressing rooms; and then further back into the depths of the basement an old, massive boiler still stands as a stark reminder of days gone by when coal-fired boilers kept the theater warm and water-washed-air cooled the interior.

But let's go back and peek inside those dressing rooms. Graffiti from the '20s, '30s, and '40s dot the walls, and carved initials of long-gone actors and musicians are scribbled into the wood facings and plaster walls.

What memories do these walls hold? Some of the earliest stories of paranormal occurrences have to do with sounds emanating from these dressing rooms, where vaudeville actors dressed.

Just past the dressing rooms, farther down under the stage, is a large, open room with a door to the orchestra pit. As you stand and look around, it might seem as if you are stepping back in time. On the east side of the room is a door to the mechanical room where the blower to the pipe organ is located, and sometimes visitors can hear a faint sound whistling through the pipes, even though the organ has been disconnected for years.

Farther along the hallway, past the vaudeville dressing rooms, the old, metal doors separating the abandoned heating and cooling systems, creak and drag on the concrete floor as they are opened. They have an eerie, haunting sound, but the doors' rusty hinges and dragging noises on the floor don't seem to impede them from opening without cause. The bare light-bulbs flicker, and creaking sounds permeate the area.

A short walk to the back of the far west wall—behind the huge antique boiler—there is a door that seemingly leads to nowhere. Open this door and you will see a small, dusty room with a dirt floor and then a blank wall that is certainly one of the more puzzling features found in the theater. The plaster on the north wall seems patched and filled in. Was there a door where the newer plaster is on the wall? A look into the room with its dirt floor only seems to raise more questions. What was this room used for, and why is there a dirt floor?

Undoubtedly, this room was part of some larger something. Of course, many of El Dorado's older citizens will swear there was an outside door that led to the entrance of the tunnel, which was rumored to be covered up on Halloween night in 1931 after a tragic accident. This small room—where you can almost touch all the thick walls—is the most soundproof spot in the theater. But strangely enough, sounds have reportedly been heard coming from behind the supposedly solid north wall, which directly faces the theater's basement. And many people have commented about what seems to be the presence of something in this small room, where a strange smell—perfume or a cigar—has often been reported.

What is *behind* the wall? Is it the sealed entrance to the notorious tunnel to the courthouse?

The old theater has so many nooks and crannies that an investigation of all the reported paranormal occurrences is impossible. However, even if only 10 percent of the stories and rumors that have been attributed to this historic theater hold a grain of truth, then this old building holds secrets that would shock the sanest individual. This theater and the blocks surrounding it have seen their share of mayhem, love, and lust in their almost 90 years of existence.

The walls have stories and, from the comments of workers and theater patrons, someone, something, or maybe several dozen ghosts are trying to make themselves known. At least that's what many people think.

As we explore the rumors and recount the old stories that have been passed down from generation to generation, I think you will have a better grasp of this special theater—the haunted Rialto.

Before we go into the details of the numerous paranormal—supernatural occurrences that have been recorded, let's take a quick paranormal tour of the building and briefly touch on some of the apparitions and horrific incidents that have made themselves known to various patrons and workers.

Many stories are related from the projectionists who peered out of the booth to see the lust on "whores' row" (the last row of seats in the middle of the balcony away from the sidewall lights) as well as nightly mayhem from the 1920s that included fights, and, yes, murders that took place in the upper reaches of the balcony. These projectionists, who may have been paid off to say some woman was drunk or that a murder was an accident, may have observed the prostitute who fell—or was pushed—over the balcony rail to fall 50 feet to her death on the concrete floor of the main auditorium below.

Was the grisly murder of another 'lady of the evening' observed by the projectionist? We have heard a rumor that after the last show one night, when the lights were turned on for the cleanup crew, workers found a young, pregnant prostitute with her throat cut lying against the back wall of the balcony.

The tales of paranormal occurrences reported aren't confined to the interior of the building. The south end of the theater is only a few hundred yards from the old railroad station and the ancient church cemetery, where Confederate soldiers lie in unmarked graves beside young women and children who were victims of Yellow Fever, and the desecrated slave cemetery is only a stone's throw away from this spot.

On Halloween, the historical society commemorates the lives of many of the more famous El Dorado citizens by having actors and actresses dress in costumes and stand near the grave markers in the historic Presbyterian Cemetery to tell the story of well-known El Dorado residents who are buried there. And of course, the actors are quick to tell you strange stories about paranormal sightings around the old cemetery. But, the grisly secret of the old slave cemetery is never mentioned.

Where are the graves of the hundreds of slaves? What happened to them? Well, we'll look into that dark secret, hidden away for over 90 years, later in this book.

Candles placed around ancient tombstones and the elaborate wrought-iron fences and gates give the whole cemetery an eerie presence on Halloween, reflecting its checkered past. Why did the South Arkansas Historical Society pick All Hallows' Eve to highlight the lives of early El Dorado settlers? Why do the men and women who portray early residents of the city refuse to go into certain sections of the graveyard unaccompanied?

Ask them and they will tell you about sounds and balls of light that seem to drift over the graves, especially toward the back of the cemetery. Are these apparitions trying to convey a dark secret, one long hidden from the public? A secret so despicable that just the mention of it would send a chill up the spine the average citizen. Maybe someone, or something, is calling out about the rumored desecration that occurred outside the back iron fence of the graveyard.

We have talked about the back of the theater, but how about the front?

The Rialto faces Cedar Street and, during the boom, Mrs. Davis's Hotel was a half block west of the theater entrance. Evidently, it was quite a rowdy place. To quote Mrs. Jenkins, one of the musicians who played for silent movies: *"When we left the theater, (almost midnight) we had to walk down the middle of the street to avoid being hit. If we walked on the sidewalk next to the buildings we could have been hurt by objects or people being thrown out the windows."*

The bodies that Mrs. Jenkins talked about were men—and maybe a few prostitutes—who were thrown from windows on the second or third floor of the Davis Hotel. Naturally, police records from the early '20s have nothing to say about any injuries or deaths of individuals due to being tossed out hotel windows.

That is an actual quote, however, from an eyewitness who worked for years in the old Rialto. Her descriptions of the wild and lawless days of the boom, give you a hint of the mayhem that occurred during the early 1920s. Stories abound about the violence that spilled over from the street into the theater, and the tales of bodies that were picked up in the rear of the theater after a particularly wild weekend are legendary. Police reports involving the area near the theater called Hamburger Row are almost nonexistent, because it seems there were two standards for the law in El Dorado during the early 1920s.

13

THE PROJECTIONISTS—JACK RICHARDSON

One of the most vivid scenes that psychic Carol Pate observed during her visit was that of a projectionist who seemed to have spents hours and hours in the theater and considered the projection booth his territory.

On Thursday, Dec. 19, 1985, the "*El Dorado News-Times*" printed an interview with Jack Richardson, who was the Rialto projectionist for longer than anyone else. This material below includes excerpts from that interview. I have added this material to give readers an understanding of how the theater prospered during its heyday.

***

For Jack Richardson, memories of the Rialto Theater spanned 26 years. In 1948, Richardson discarded dreams of being a major league baseball player to become a projectionist at the Rialto. From 1948 to 1974, he was the man who performed the technical tasks necessary to transform the theater into something fresh from Hollywood's imagination.

Richardson said he considered his job a *"prestige position in one of the five best showplaces in the South. Outside (of) it being a livelihood, I felt like I was doing my part in contributing to the community—running the show for people to enjoy."*

Richardson stated that theaters used to be much more formal, complete with ushers to show patrons to their seats. *"There weren't many TV's in the late forties and fifties." Richardson said. "Movies were the going pastime. To satisfy a good movie fan you needed good sound and no breaks in the film—that would keep them coming back."*

Film preparation, according to Richardson, was a painstaking task that required a lot of work.

"I took extra care for the first run of the film, which was not for the audience but to identify weak spots in light and sound and possible breakage points. If a dying man was whispering his last words on the screen, I would turn up the sound; for a band of attacking Indians, I would turn the sound down."

From his unique perspective in a land-bound theater like the Rialto, Richardson recalled a late '50s incident comparable to one of today's television bloopers.

"We paged patrons by projecting their names onto the screen," he said. "Doctors, in particular, were likely to be paged during a movie. In one Biblical epic, the Pharaoh was dying and Yul Brenner was taking over. Everyone on the theater was very quiet.

"In the middle of the dramatic death scene— I wasn't paying attention to what was going on the screen at the time—I flashed a local doctor's name on the screen, and it brought the house down. It was a doctor everyone was familiar with, as if a Union County doctor was gonna get the Pharaoh well."

The projection booth at the Rialto also doubled as an aviary for El Dorado's downtown pigeon population. Richardson recalled how one pigeon got in on the act during a horror movie when a screeching audience frightened the bird from its perch in the rear of the balcony. *"When the audience started screaming, the pigeon started cooing loudly and flying directly toward the screen with its shadow being projected onto the screen. You can imagine how that frightened the audience!"*

A regular Rialto customer that Richardson remembers was a woman he referred to as 9:40 Nell. *"9:40 Nell came like clockwork to the 9:40 movie on Wednesday and Sunday nights. That's when we changed the movies; every Wednesday and Sunday you could set your watch by Nell."*

For 26 years, Jack Richardson was the man behind the scenes at the Rialto Theater, El Dorado's palace for Hollywood's ethereal royalty. Richardson remembers that someone once said, "A projectionist is a man who knows no applause."

Richardson did get "silent applause," however, when El Dorado's audiences kept returning to the Rialto, most unaware of his painstaking efforts to provide them with "the best show in town as one of the five top theaters in the South." (End of newspaper article.)

***

I have included the information about Jack Richardson because Carol Pate, the renowned psychic, positively identified him when she toured the Rialto. Especially, when she went into the projection booth did she recognize his spirit. Her description of the spirit—down to the cap he was wearing—matches Jack Richardson to a T. As Pate made her rounds and entered the projection booth, "Jack" made himself known to her and objected to her being there. He even told her to leave, saying, *"You don't belong here."*

This spirit is one of the most prevalent apparitions present in the theater. Pate discerned that he was not only the projectionist, but a handyman who spent a lot of time in the theater. As she noted, "Jack" actually lived in the theater for a time, which is true.

14

THE TUNNEL

THE roaring oil boom of the 1920s spawned many stories, but none is more popular and told more often than the rumor of The Tunnel. Ah, yes, the mysterious tunnel: of all the stories and rumors that have swirled around the Rialto Theater and downtown El Dorado, perhaps the story about a secret tunnel connecting the basement of the courthouse to the basement of the Rialto Theater is the most prevalent.

Speculation about the rumored tunnel's use, and speculation about its construction, have been fodder for many a conversation around town. Old men have sworn they walked through the tunnel—and stories that have drifted through El Dorado about what happened in the basement of the courthouse and in the basement of the Rialto leading into the tunnel have been shocking. Of course, even the men who claimed to have walked through the tunnel turn mute when further questions are asked. Yes, it seems the rumor of the tunnel is something "old El Dorado" wants to keep swept under the rug.

I wonder why? Or is the tunnel just a wild rumor?

Today, in the basement of the Rialto Theater, there is a low, 4-foot door behind the east stairs that lead from the main auditorium to the downstairs vaudeville dressing rooms. A closer look makes you wonder if this could be the entrance to the tunnel. However, even though a person can enter the supposed tunnel there, it only extends 50 feet. A bricked-up wall stops further exploration of this short piece of tunnel.

This 50-foot section extends due north toward the courthouse. However, there's no trace of the tunnel on the south, plastered wall in the courthouse basement. A smooth, plastered wall hides any trace of the tunnel.

Naturally, if there was a tunnel between the Rialto and the courthouse sometime during the past, it begs the question: Why was the tunnel constructed, and who used it?

In order for us to understand the need for a tunnel, we have to look at what was happening in the area around the old theater when rumors say the tunnel was completed. From stories that have filtered back from the very early 1920s, and from tales that have been handed down from family to family, we believe the tunnel was first constructed when the old 1921 and 1925 Rialto Theaters were in operation. Evidently, during construction of the first Rialto Theater in the early 1920s, the need for a tunnel to the courthouse was proposed as a way to travel from the safety of the courthouse square to the Hamburger Row "Entertainment District" without walking down the most dangerous 200-yards of street in the town—the dark alleyways and unlit sidewalks where hijackers lurked.

The rumor goes something like this: Construction, work began in 1921 and the passageway was in use by the first part of 1922. The workers dug the tunnel from the basement of the old, redbrick Victorian courthouse and ended up in the basement of the old 1921 Rialto Theater, which was new at the time. In 1928 and '29, after the new theater and new courthouse were built, the tunnel was enlarged and used until it was secretly sealed off.

Some whispered gossip says it was on Halloween night, 1931, after a tragic accident that the tunnel was sealed off... at least that's the story that has made the rounds in El Dorado. I think the early 1930s is probably a good guess as to when the tunnel was closed and the entranceways bricked off. I have not been able come up with any stories or even rumors about the tunnel being used after that time. All of the accounts point to the tunnel being in use for about 10 years after construction was finished in 1922.

However, based on the stories passed down from several generations, the original tunnel, built in 1922, was probably improved and enlarged when the new Rialto Theater was built in 1928-29. It seems the original tunnel, probably constructed in 1922 before the new theater was built, was poorly constructed, and when the new theater was built it was improved.

It's easy to understand why some of the citizens of El Dorado wanted a tunnel. So in order to see the need for a safe tunnel, we need to look at the area surrounding the Rialto.

It was a time and a moment that has been set in bronze on the Oil Heritage Park monuments across from the Rialto. On Jan. 10, 1921, at 4 p.m. a booming gusher, whose spewing oil could be seen from downtown El Dorado, signaled the start of the boom. The town went wild.

During the early, lawless days of the oil boom, prostitution and open gambling flourished along Hamburger Row and the adjacent streets south of the courthouse square. The Rialto is only half a block from this infamous street, and stories of prostitutes frequenting the Rialto are numerous. The city police department seemed to have two standards during the early '20s. There were frequent patrols, for example, around the courthouse square, where fashionable ladies shopped, and the prostitutes, drug dealers, and other rowdies were not welcome. But only a block away, there was a different standard.

In the first two years of the oil boom, a walk down South Washington Avenue south from the courthouse square toward the railroad station would shock your senses. As you passed the Garrett Hotel, all semblances of law and order quickly disappeared. Prostitutes solicited, gambling houses lined the street, saloons were stacked with wall-to-wall whiskey, and drug dealers pulled your sleeve offering you their wares.

Of course, the barrelhouses with their whiskey, gambling, and prostitutes were frequented by some of the lowest cast of individuals who preyed on the oil boom throngs, and robbery and murder were a common occurrence. However, the oil boom trash were not the only ones who frequented the street; many of El Dorado's leading citizens also found their entertainment there, and as the lawlessness spun out of control during the early '20s, these men became afraid to venture down Hamburger Row after dark.

It was during that era that we first hear of the tunnel and its use. Rumors about the men who built the tunnel include a group of El Dorado's most prominent citizens. They had become rich from the oil boom, and they still wanted the barrelhouse entertainment but they were afraid to venture down Hamburger Row after dark to gamble, visit prostitutes, and drink moonshine.

Yes, it was a matter of safety. The alleyways between Main Street and Hamburger Row were notorious hangouts for the gangs of hijackers, who robbed and murdered hundreds of men a month. By bypassing these alleyways, the men could reach Cedar Street and South Washington Avenue (Hamburger Row) safely.

It was during the same time period that the new Rialto and the current courthouse were constructed. There is a persistent story of how, during construction of the Rialto, influential citizens who frequented the courthouse got together and enlarged an existing tunnel between the basement of the Rialto and the basement of the courthouse. According to several comments that I would classify as rumored history, the local jail furnished a truckload of inmates that worked at night digging the tunnel.

According to some sketchy tales from older members of the community, the plan was simple: Bring the gambling, whiskey, and women from the Rialto basement through a tunnel to the basement of the courthouse, where two lavish rooms were set up. The men who financed this operation could go in to the courthouse basement, sit back and wait for their entertainment of the night, which would be brought to them via the Rialto tunnel, as it was called. Or if they felt especially brave, they could travel from the courthouse to the Rialto through the tunnel and bypass a stretch of dangerous real estate. At the end of the tunnel, they could walk out of the Rialto Theater into the midst of the Hamburger Row's "Entertainment District."

Speculation is that traffic in the tunnel went both ways: Prostitutes from the barrelhouses on Hamburger Row began to come to movies at the Rialto and, during the show, would go to the basement and walk through the tunnel to the courthouse where they would drink and service the men waiting for them. However, some sources say that after only a few weeks, the women began to complain about voices and noises in the tunnel, and soon they were refusing to enter the tunnel without a man accompanying them.

Questions have swirled around the community for years: If there was a tunnel, then why was it closed, and what happened to make some of the leading citizens of the community want to seal it off? Naturally, since stories about the tunnel lack any documentation, my accounts about it are based on rumors and very little else.

It does seem, however, from my research, that these rumors about the tunnel first started in 1922 and continued until the early 1930s. Many have wondered not only about the tunnel, but also the *"hush, hush,"* concerning the reason it was sealed off. My theory is that only a significant tragedy could have provoked such a drastic step as to seal off the tunnel, and attempt to cover up the reason. But if a tragedy *did* occur, then how could law enforcement officials of the time manage to cover it up?

I believe it stands to reason that if the victims were workers from the barrelhouses or prostitutes from the brothels, then in 1922, on lawless Hamburger Row, who would care if they perished in a tunnel cave-in? In the 1920s, the hundreds of murders committed by criminals who preyed on the oilfield workers and others, were largely ignored by the town. So it makes perfect sense to believe some tragedy occurred that was dramatic enough to force the tunnel to be sealed off, and even its former existence to be denied. The mysterious tunnel, denied by many of the current citizens of El Dorado, is a matter of speculation and its disappearance is something that many of El Dorado's older citizens refuse to talk about.

There are stories that after the new Rialto was constructed, the old tunnel was carefully preserved and a special door from the alley behind the theater was built to allow people to go directly from the alleyway through the basement of the theater and into the tunnel. It is also rumored that the notorious Slivertop, a barrelhouse owner whose hair had turned prematurely gray, was the man who supplied entertainment to the men who waited in the courthouse. The door from the back of the Rialto into the basement was manned by "Big Ed" a giant of a man, 6 feet 8 inches tall and weighing over 300 pounds. He kept the dope dealers, prostitutes, and gamblers under control and only let in the men and women who had a chit from Silvertop's Barrelhouse.

As you might imagine, even with Big Ed occasionally there to maintain order, the alley behind the Rialto became a dangerous place and many a man and woman met their death from a dope deal gone bad or ended up hijacked and knifed, as it was known back then.

But back to the theater and to the rear of the building: Today it seems to be very ordinary—only a thick metal door, with a faded sign saying "Concessions" gives a hint of what may lurk here. Did this ancient, dented-and-scratched door lead to the inner secret of the Rialto? Was it a meeting place for the dope peddlers of the oil boom and the prostitutes who would go through the door (or one beside it that has been bricked over) and into the basement of the theater? And then through the door into the rumored tunnel to walk those 200 yards underground to the basement of the courthouse where a lavish room, and some of the leading citizens of El Dorado awaited them?

Of course, if you stand there by the door looking south toward the cemetery and the train station, it's not hard to understand why stories have abounded about this eerie, hidden section of town. Did the scratches on the concession—tunnel door come from the "colored" ghosts whose graves were bulldozed to make room for the new train station? Did the clandestine dope peddling and prostitution that occurred at the back of the theater, sometimes end up in violence? We only know one thing for sure: The mortuary wagon picked up numerous bodies from this area, and theater workers over the years have told some strange tales. Stories of bloodcurdling screams and one of a dying young woman that managed to crawl around to the front of the building and, before she died, screamed out a story so violent and horrible that the theater manager instructed workers never to talk about it.

As the oil boom violence continued, theater management began to hire guards to patrol the back of the theater and the upper part of the balcony where most of the assaults happened. However, some of the guards quit, complaining of strange calls for help and an eerie, overpowering presence of something near the alleyway concession door. Bright lights were installed on the corners of the building, guards were on the corners, and guards were instructed not to go to the back of the theater under any circumstances.

The story below is one wild, possible theory of what happened that caused the tunnel to be sealed off.

Ah, yes, All Hallows Eve, when countries around the world pay homage to the dead and their spirits that still drift in and out of our lives. We call it Halloween and today it seems to be a time for young children to receive candy for wearing outlandish costumes. However, in El Dorado's not-so-distant past, Oct. 31, 1931, events occurred that made the population of El Dorado shudder… at least to those who knew the awful tragedy that occurred that night. It was an October night that was unseasonably cold, and a bitter north wind made any trip outside unbearable. That Halloween it was an eerie moonless night, and almost all the business in downtown El Dorado had closed for the night as an early cloud-induced darkness enveloped the community.

In the basement of the courthouse, a wood-burning fireplace was filled with pine kindling, which made a very hot fire, and a crowd of men gathered to partake of a batch of moonshine the sheriff had recently confiscated.

It was after 11 o'clock and the drinking and general carousing had reached its peak when someone decided the party needed some ladies to liven things up. They decided to invite over prostitutes from one of the brothels for more festivities. The brothels and their girls were a holdover from the roaring oil boom of the 1920s, and the girls were on a circuit that took them to Texarkana, Hot Springs, Jackson (Mississippi),and then back to El Dorado.

When the phones rang at one of the brothels, the girls were all invited to the courthouse to celebrate. "The more the merrier," said the caller when he was told that seven girls would make the walk through the tunnel to the courthouse. The girls, dressed in the skimpiest of clothes, bundled up the best they could and hurried out the hotel door.

The sight of seven women, in high heels, heavily made up and wearing costumes reminiscent of the 1920s must have been a sight to behold. They slipped into the basement of the Rialto through the back "concession" door.

The Rialto and its tunnel was well known by these girls, and they had all made the trek many times. When the oil boom started in 1920, the area of South Washington Avenue called Hamburger Row developed the well-earned reputation of being extremely dangerous. The girls had been through the tunnel many times to meet men in the basement of the courthouse, since the men were afraid to venture down South Washington Avenue after dark. Many reports have been handed down of scantily dressed girls scurrying across South Washington Avenue accompanied by escorts, and disappearing into the back of the theater, a block away.

As soon as they were all huddled in the basement and their guard had left, the attendant on duty opened the door to the tunnel. At first, the girls were hesitant because the lights that had been strung in the tunnel had failed, and the only illumination was from a coal-oil lantern held by the attendant. They milled around in the basement of the Rialto until one of the courthouse workers appeared, and, with a few extra dollars and the promise of hundreds more, he led a contingent of seven young women into the dark tunnel.

There is some confusion as to what happened next. According to some stories, a groan was heard and then a gust of wind, from nobody knows where, blew out the coal-oil lamp, and the tunnel was filled with seven women screaming their lungs out. However, a couple of the girls said the courthouse worker deliberately extinguished the lamp to fool around with one of the girls. But what happened when the tunnel was dark, with a cold wind blowing through it, is hard to describe.

As the girls, led by the attendant, made their way through the tunnel they linked themselves together by holding on to the back of each other's dresses. Soon the string of girls was well into the tunnel, and they were walking gingerly on the rough-hewn planks that made up the floor and brushing the dirt walls as they stumbled on toward the courthouse.

The roof of the tunnel was supported by beams and timbers spaced every 6 feet, with one, long, horizontal timber tying them together. It was a very slipshod bit of tunnel construction, and minor cave-ins had already occurred several times since it was built.

After each cave-in, the sheriff would bring prisoners in to clean out the fallen timbers and shore up the tunnel again. But as the years passed, conditions inside the tunnel had deteriorated and the lights that went out that night were just considered to be one more problem. Evidently, however, the problem with the lights indicated more of a problem than anyone anticipated, and when the girls and their attendant reached the midpoint of the tunnel, the man accompanying the girls found a timber had slipped off from the wall and was blocking the way. He reached down and pulled it aside, triggering a chain reaction, and the tunnel began to collapse. Timbers and dirt gradually covered the girls' escort, and then the girls, themselves, were enveloped.

There was a panic to escape but the falling timbers and crumbling dirt engulfed girl after girl until only the last two made it back to the basement of the Rialto. Those two, terror-stricken girls ran out of the theater screaming hysterically, and soon the men from the courthouse had rushed down to the theater and entered the tunnel to begin a rescue.

What they found is still whispered about in El Dorado. The tunnel had collapsed some hundred feet from the Rialto basement entrance and the searchers were met with a wall of dirt and timbers.. Of course, initially, the men started to dig and try to clean out the debris, but it soon became obvious that any movement of timber or dirt put the remainder of the open tunnel in danger. After a meeting with the sheriff and police chief, a secret plan was hatched.

Since all the girls lost were prostitutes, and the only man killed was someone who worked for a brothel, the men decided to seal up both ends of the tunnel and swear each other to secrecy. After all, the death of five girls and one man in a secret tunnel to the courthouse would have ruined the reputation of a number of El Dorado's leading citizens.

Well, that's just one of the many speculations about what happened to the mysterious tunnel. However, the often-repeated tale of the tunnel connecting the basement of the courthouse to the basement of the Rialto may not be all of the story.

Recently I heard a rumor about another tunnel, and this tunnel also starts in the basement of the Rialto, but instead of going to the courthouse it goes to the basement of the Randolph Hotel. I have only heard speculation about this tunnel from one individual, but because of the circumstances during the mid to late 1920s it seems to have some validity.

After the Randolph Hotel was constructed and the Petroleum Club was opened, the hotel was frequented by numerous prostitutes. Many witnesses documented these "Girls of the Randolph." And, supposedly, this secondary tunnel was constructed to keep private the visits of prominent businessmen, who did not wish to be seen going in and out of the hotel.

I have no idea if there is anything to this rumor, but I think it's very possible. The Rialto Theater and the basement of the hotel are so close that a tunnel would only have had to be extended about 170 feet or less to connect the two. By entering the Rialto to ostensibly attend a picture show, a businessman could walk to the basement of the theater and minutes later be inside the hotel. The sight of a businessman entering the Randolph was sure to cause rumors of a tryst with the "girls," as noted in one of my interviews with a lady who happened to see a very prominent city leader entering the hotel with one of the "ladies of the night" on his arm.

Actually, this tunnel makes more since than the tunnel to the courthouse because of the distance involved and the reason for having it. However, maybe neither tunnel ever existed—or maybe not only were there two tunnels but possibly a third one, as rumors have it, extending to the Presbyterian Cemetery on South Washington Avenue. (The story behind this possible tunnel is that it was used to take hanged criminals from the gallows to the paupers' cemetery behind the Presbyterian Cemetery.

Sometime in the future, when ground-penetrating technology is available, we will be able to tell if these tunnels actually exist.

15

LADIES AND SCOUNDRELS

El Dorado has always had its share of colorful men and women. The list is certainly varied, and it includes a man who got his start in the oil boom of the 1920s and became the richest man in the world. But there were as many colorful women as there were men, and one of the most noted was:

Myrtelle McWilliams

In 1925, at the height of the South Arkansas oil boom, J. W. and Myrtle McWilliams constructed a large Mediterranean-influenced home at 323 West Oak St. just two blocks from the center of town. Myrtle would live in this house for more than 50 years, and during that time, she became El Dorado's consummate hostess.

The McWilliams' spacious, brick home was designed with open archways connecting the downstairs rooms to allow easier access for the numerous guests that attended Myrtle's parties. Her Dec. 23 Christmas party, for example, was the ultimate social event of the season, and to be left off of Myrtle's invitation list brought many a young, would-be socialite to tears.

Myrtle remained Myrtle until later in life when she began traveling. Over the years, Myrtle confided to her friends that she had never liked the name Myrtle, and so when she began to go on cruises after the death of her husband, she introduced herself as Myrtelle. She liked it so much that after a few years she legally changed her name from Myrtle to Myrtelle. She was an attractive, outgoing sensual woman who loved bridge, parties, and...men.

Boarding school teachers:

Very soon, after the McWilliams moved into their new home, they were asked to board two, new, single female schoolteachers. The ongoing oil boom had created a dire shortage of housing, and the school system desperately needed additional teachers.

The McWilliamses, being stalwart citizens of the community, opened their home to these teachers. However, they were aware of the dangers of going into town, even to the grocery store, so Myrtelle came up with an ingenious way to assure the girls' safety.

The McWilliams home is only a few blocks from downtown. But with the influx of thousands of oilfield workers, a single, young woman just walking downtown might well be accosted, touched, or propositioned. This was Myrtelle's solution: When a teacher went downtown after school, Myrtelle handed them a large doll wrapped in a blanket. To the oilfield workers, it seemed as if the women were carrying babies, and none of the teachers were ever harassed.

The Samples Department Store delivery boy:

Edwin Alderson, a former Union County judge and good friend of mine, was a delivery boy for Samples during the early 1950s. One day, he stopped by Myrtelle's house to make a delivery and knocked on the front door. Myrtelle, who considered herself the social queen of El Dorado, came to the door.

"Mrs. McWilliams, I have a package from Samples for you."

"I'm sorry, Edwin, but we only take deliveries at the back door."

Edwin walked around back and Myrtelle opened the back door and took the delivery.

"Thank you, Edwin, and tell your mother, I said hello."

You would think a fine department store and a young man from a prominent family would know better than to try to deliver to the front door.

Men Friends

Evidently, starting early in her marriage, Myrtelle found the company of other men irresistible. That weakness created quite a stir in town. She was a full-figured woman who knew how to use her sexuality, and, as some of Myrtelle's friends will tell you, she didn't hesitate to use her obvious charms to attract men. A touch, nudge, or kiss in the hall during one of her frequent parties was usually enough to have the lucky or unlucky man—if he happened to get caught—rendezvous with her while J. W. was in town on away on business.

However, there were times when Myrtelle's propensity for the opposite sex became fraught with danger. One such incident happened when J. W. was supposedly out of town.

Tragedy in the bedroom:

It seems, according to stories I've heard, J. W. must have become suspicious of Myrtelle's men friends, and he evidently created a situation where she could invite her current lover over for a tryst. J. W. announced he would be out of town on business until late that night and Myrtelle should not wait supper on him.

It was mid-afternoon when her lover arrived, and they immediately went upstairs to her bedroom and began to make love. It must have been quite a surprise to both of them that afternoon when J. W. kicked her bedroom door open and found them in a very compromising position.

J. W., who carried a gun because of the rough crowd that came with the oil boom, pulled his gun and began firing at the couple while they were still in bed. He hit Myrtelle's lover who staggered out the bedroom door, collapsed on the upstairs landing, and died from the gunshot wound.

No charges were filed, and Myrtelle and J. W. made up and continued their marriage.

I was buying antiques in the late 1980s, and discovered this very bed, which was sold at Melvin Bell's Antique Store bankruptcy auction in Little Rock. The auctioneer noted the bullet hole in the headboard and recounted the above story.

The shot from the upstairs bedroom window:

Evidently, sometime later in life, after J. W. died, Myrtelle didn't lose her desire to be with men, and she seemingly had a particular thing for doctors. Several years after J. W. died, Myrtelle was having a torrid affair with a married, local physician. This doctor had an office across the street from Myrtelle's house, and the parking lot for the clinic was directly across from the McWilliams house. When Myrtelle found out the doctor was also having an affair with another El Dorado lady, she was incensed.

"I'll teach him to two-time me!" she vowed.

The next morning, Myrtelle loaded her pistol and stood at an open bedroom window with a clear view of the parking lot across the street. She was waiting on her doctor-lover to come to work. When he pulled up in the parking lot and stepped out of his car, Myrtelle calmly raised her .38-caliber pistol and began firing. A half-dozen shots rang out, hitting the pavement, car, and finally the doctor. She managed to wound the doctor, but his wounds were not fatal.

Evidently, that ended the affair. Myrtelle was never charged with attempted murder or any crime, for that matter, and "Old" El Dorado neatly covered up that incident as they did so many of the other past black marks on the community.

I never knew Myrtelle, but I wished I had. The Myrtelle's of this world are the spice that makes life in a small town bearable.

Ghosts in Myrtelle's House

You might expect, considering the colorful and tragic history surrounding Myrtelle's House, that paranormal occurrences would be noted. And yes, there have been numerous accounts by recent guests from Union Square Guest Quarters. Several men have refused to stay there again after encountering unexplained footsteps on the stairwell and a persistent feeling that someone is watching them. Other guests have commented about hearing voices from empty rooms or moaning on the upstairs landing next to the room where they were staying.

In my opinion, the tragic shooting that occurred in the upstairs bedroom is related to the haunting of the house. After all, most of the paranormal occurrences documented in this book have been associated with murders or violent deaths. It seems to me that one of Myrtelle's lovers haunts the house.

Barrelhouse Sue

Yes, El Dorado has had its share of colorful women almost from the founding of the town. In the 1920s oil boom, there were a number of infamous ladies who made living in the boomtown squalor a little more pleasant. And one of the most unusual was Barrelhouse Sue, a prostitute who not only provided her services, but actually owned several brothels.

She was "working" in north Louisiana when oil was discovered in South Arkansas, and as the Arkansas boom picked up steam, Sue moved her business to El Dorado's Hamburger Row. During the early 1920s, she made quite a name for herself.

According to eyewitnesses, Barrelhouse Sue was very attractive, a great businesswoman, and tough as nails. There are numerous accounts, for example, of her decking obnoxious, drunk roughnecks with a right cross that packed a devastating wallop.

Sue moved with the boom, and when new, huge wells announced the Smackover Field was going to be the biggest thing in South Arkansas, she moved to Smackover and, a year later as new wells moved the boom north, traveled five miles to the village of Louann.

Although Sue was a rough-and-tumble woman when she was running her brothels, she had a refined side, and she frequently attended social events organized by South Arkansas ladies. According to oral histories, she was not only tolerated, she was also cordially accepted and respected by some of the most socially active women of the South Arkansas communities. There are stories about her charitable giving, as well as her church attendance.

However, Sue's career ended one night at her barrelhouse in Louann, when she met her future husband. Evidently, it was almost love at first sight for both because Sue left with him soon after that. They got married and raised a family, and she retired as El Dorado's the most famous oil-boom prostitute.

Two-Shot Blondie

However, there were other notorious madams, who operated brothels on Hamburger Row, and one, with a most unusual nickname, was Two-Shot Blondie. Evidently, the name Two-Shot Blondie came from the woman's stark-white, blonde hair, and her ability to knock down a couple of whiskey shots. When a prospective customer offered to buy her a drink, it always turned out to be two.

As a madam she prided herself by importing the most attractive prostitutes available, and as a sidelight to her business, Two-Shot Blondie sold moonshine. She even had a deliveryman named Oscar who delivered her girls and moonshine to the oilfields in South Arkansas.

Recently, during an interview with the current owner of the building that once housed The Crystal Hotel, a prostitute named Blondie was mentioned as being one of the working girls who was especially well known. Evidently, if this Blondie and Two-Shot Blondie are the same woman, she initially worked at The Crystal Hotel, and, from other information I've gleaned, she later became a madam or maybe even the owner of a brothel.

GENTLEMEN AND SCOUNDRELS

H. L. Hunt

Haroldson Lafayette (H. L.) Hunt arrived in El Dorado from Lake Village, Arkansas, in the spring of 1921, shortly after the Busey Well came in. According to some of Hunt's associates, the first thing Hunt said, as he looked at the throngs of men crowding the streets was, *"Give me a deck of card and some poker chips."*

H.L. Hunt was an accomplished poker player, and immediately began playing at one of the local barrelhouses. Evidently, he was extremely successful, because he quickly became the owner of one of them. In fact, it was in a poker game in his own gambling house that Hunt won an oil lease in the El Dorado East Field, and after begging, borrowing, and hocking nearly everything he had, he drilled a well on the lease. It was a booming gusher, and H. L. Hunt was on his way to being a millionaire.

It was about that time when Hunt shut down his gambling establishment. According to sources, at midnight one Saturday, when the place was packed with gamblers, some 40 members of the Klu Klux Klan made a midnight call. The masked riders stopped in front of the barrelhouse and the Klan leader dismounted and walked in.

"Mr. Hunt!" he shouted. "I would like to have a word with you!"

Everyone stopped what they were doing and looked at the masked man as H. L. Hunt walked up and stood about 6 feet in front of the Klan leader.

"I have a message for you, Mr. Hunt!" he boomed. "You either close this place down, or face the consequences!"

Hunt never said a word, and the Klansman turned and left. Hunt stood at the door and watched the torch-bearing Klansmen ride off. He closed his barrelhouse shortly after that incident.

After the visit from the Klan, H. L. Hunt began speculating in oil and gas leases sold in the lobby of the Garrett Hotel. Soon he was buying working interest in new wells, and after being a successful investor, he began to operate and become a promoter of his own wells. Hunt made his first million dollars in South Arkansas and built a large mansion in the middle of a city block in the best neighborhood in town.

After the fabulous East Texas Field was discovered, Hunt parlayed his Arkansas holdings into hundreds of millions as he skillfully out-traded "Dad" Joiner in an all-night hotel room session, and came away with most of Joiner's stake in the huge East Texas Field.

Of course, any story about H. L. Hunt wouldn't be complete without mentioning his several wives. After Hunt's big strike in the East El Dorado Field, he traded and bought leases in the new Smackover Field. There, he continued his streak of luck with well after well, and became wealthy. He also became what seemed to be a devoted family man, married with four children.

During those early years in El Dorado, Hunt courted and, according to the court testimony of his "wife," Frania Tye, married her in Florida. Frania bore Hunt four children—while he was still married to Lyda, his legal, first wife.

After Lyda's death, he married Ruth Ray and that union also produced four children. H. L. Hunt was, by now, the father of 15 children. Scoundrel or gentlemen? Maybe a little of both.

Alvin "Titanic" Thompson and H. L. Hunt

During the early days of the boom, a noted con man by the name of Alvin "Titanic" Thompson arrived in El Dorado. He had grown up in Rogers, Arkansas, and reportedly had ties to organized crime in Hot Springs, Arkansas, and New York City. Rumor has it, he received his nickname "Titanic" after someone commented, "Everyone he plays he sinks like the Titanic."

Thompson was an accomplished golfer, an expert shooter, and an unbelievably skillful gambler. After arriving in El Dorado, he won several thousand dollars in shooting matches and golf games from local residents. He was also an excellent poker player, and soon he was a regular at Hunt's barrelhouse on Hamburger Row.

After the gambler was there for only a few weeks, he opened a bookmaking establishment and did very well—that is until he got into a poker game with Hunt, the consummate poker player. Hunt backed Titanic into a poker corner, placed a huge bet, and sank Titanic, who called a huge bet and lost. (Sources say the loss was so big that he had to wire his New York associates for extra money.)

As the story goes, Titanic asked Hunt to give him a chance to win his money back; he even offered to let Hunt select the game. Hunt agreed and said, "Checkers," which shocked Titanic, but he agreed and began practicing.

A few weeks later, when the big game was only days away, Titanic discovered that Hunt was the checker-playing champion of southeast Arkansas, and spent all his spare time playing. Titanic left town without playing the big game. Scoundrel—Yes!

Pat Marr

On Sept. 7, 1923, a shocking headline appeared in the "*El Dorado Daily News*" about a prominent oilman: **Federal Agents Nab Pat Marr on Promotions.** Scoundrel? Federal agents claimed Marr made promises in his ads that he couldn't keep, and I quote the federal charges: promises "*which no human could fulfill.*" Marr ran full-page newspaper advertisements boasting of his success and encouraging local residents to invest with him and enjoy the wealth.

Sounds like a scoundrel, but let's look a little deeper. Banker Charles Murphy Sr. and prominent businessman Sam Alphin put up Marr's $25,000 bail, and Pat went back to work drilling in the South Arkansas oilfields. Well, sure I don't think Charles Murphy Sr. or Sam Alphin would bail out a scoundrel.

Now let's take a really close look at what Pat promised in those ads, **promises that reportedly** *"no human could fulfill"* He promised to drill 10 gushers; each would produce at least 5,000 barrels of oil a day, and if they didn't, he would return the investors' money. Yes, I agree; it sure seems as if Marr is promising something that would be extremely hard to do—maybe impossible.

However, after he got out on bail, Marr did drill the 10 gushers, and in fact, he exceeded people's wildest optimist expectations. And in doing so, he proved the federal indictment wrong. Pat Marr was an oilman's oilman, and his newspaper ads were over the top—but he was not a scoundrel.

16

THE CAROL PATE PSYCHIC CENTER

AS my notes about spirits and tragic events around and in the Rialto Theater became thicker, I decided to look deeper and see if someone with psychic powers could document any of the stories. To do this, I contacted Carol Pate, a noted psychic, in order to document and obtain more information concerning the many paranormal experiences that have occurred in the Rialto Theater and its environs.

Pate's credentials are superb, as one who can apparently discern the existence of spirit entities and communicate with paranormal apparitions. And her work with police and other investigative agencies is respected and known worldwide.

Pate is someone who can visualize, through energy imprints, scenes from the past. So if anyone could contact the spirits present or visualize past events in the vicinity of the Rialto Theater, Carol Pate would probably be the one.

From Carol Pate's web page:

Carol Pate was born with psychic abilities. By the age of twelve, she was working with law enforcement agencies in helping them solve cases of embezzlement, homicide and missing persons. She is now a licensed minister, a teacher and practicing psychic counselor.

In 1991, Ms. Pate was chosen as the top female psychic in the United States by the Unicorn World Coordination and the Tokyo Broadcasting Company of

Japan. She has been featured in three international documentaries, and has worked with all facets of the media in local, state, and national levels, as well as internationally. She has appeared as a guest expert on "The Geraldo Rivera Show" and has also appeared on "The Other Side", "Sighting," Unsolved Mysteries" and "Beyond Chance". Most recently on MSNBC's "The Abrams Report," "Psychic Detectives" and "Larry King Live."

Through the University of Arkansas' continuing education program, Ms. Pate taught her "ESP and the Paranormal" course for five years. She continues to conduct private workshops and seminars on a regularly scheduled basis. As time permits, she is available for speaking engagement at schools, colleges, churches, and civic organizations.

Her private practice includes working with the public on multiple levels. She has given thousands of personal readings utilizing her pschycometry talent and other psychic abilities to offer council and advice in all areas of personal concern.

Carol is an information provider and in addition to her normal caseloads, she works on more than 500 murder cases a year.

***

As soon as I contacted Pate and made an appointment for her to come and visit the Rialto, unusual things began to happen. First, several weeks before she was to arrive, Pate called and said she wanted to postpone the trip because El Dorado was supposed to have bad weather that day. Well, I pulled up the weather map and looked at the long-range forecast, and checked on the date: nothing. There was a 10 percent chance of rain and 50-degree temperatures. However, when that scheduled day rolled around, it was 32 degrees, sleeting, raining, and producing winter storm warnings. I began to think this lady really did have an insight into the supernatural.

When Pate arrived a few weeks later, we visited over lunch and then, before we went to the theater, we took her up upstairs to some rooms in a new building—rooms in which several individuals had experienced strange happenings. In rooms six and three in the Union Square Guest Quarters, a downtown executive inn, numerous guests have reported paranormal experiences.

The most vivid incident was reported by a young woman, a pharmaceutical sales representative, who was staying in room six. This lady watched TV until about 10 o'clock, turned off the bedside light, and rolled over to go to sleep. However, almost immediately, she felt someone sit down on the side of her bed, and the bed indented. She jumped up, ran down the hall, and stayed with a friend in another room.

In that room and in another room down the hall, room three, lights have come on during the night, the TV has been turned on, commodes flush, water runs—and all without explanation. It seems that something or someone wants to make themselves known.

These paranormal occurrences sure had me puzzled because the building that houses Union Square Guest Quarters is less than 10 years old. Are spirits present in a relatively new building where nothing out of the ordinary has happened during construction or since the Guest Quarters opened? However, as I later learned, spirits aren't confined to one building, but as in this case, they may have come to occupy a new building built on the site of an older building.

Pate and I visited both rooms, which had had numerous paranormal occurrences. In room six, Pate nodded and started describing the scene. Soon she was able to confirm the presence of several spirits.

The principal spirit was a young mother who seemed distraught about what she believed had been a terrible accident. She and her husband had traveled to El Dorado and taken a hotel apartment for the family, which consisted of a boy of 4 or 5, and a baby.

The mother's name is Nora Dean, Pate reported, and she is waiting for her husband to return. She has heard of an accident in the drilling of an oil well where two men were killed, and she is grieving because she believes her husband may be one of the victims of the accident.

During this period, before the discovery of oil in South Arkansas, the #1 Constantine was drilled west of town, and it encountered a strong natural gas flow and raged out of control for several weeks. Two men were killed when someone struck a match to light a cigarette. Was one of the men killed the husband Nora Dean was waiting for?

Pate described the small apartment the family had been living in, and it sure wasn't anything like the current Guest Quarters' rooms. However, in the early 1900s a large hotel named the Arcade, occupied the site. The hotel was converted into a grocery store in the 1940s and a McCroy's Five and Dime in the 1950s, and then was demolished to build new structures that still occupy the site.

One of these buildings is now the Union Square Guest Quarters, and all are built on the site of the old Arcade Hotel, which along with rooms for rent offered small apartments by the month.

Are these spirits waiting for the returning husband and father from the old hotel? I'll be honest: I was a little skeptical at first, and although I made notes, in my mind there was a lot of doubt about what Pate described to me. I needed a lot more convincing before giving my approval.

But little did I know that other startling revelations were about to shed light on these paranormal occurrences, and—quite honestly—make a believer out of me. In fact, it would come from another room just down the hall, in room three.

That room in the Guest Quarters had also been cited as having disturbing paranormal occurrences. Guests staying there, for example, have called to question strange odors, lights that mysteriously turn on, or the smell of smoke. Some of our regular guests won't even stay in the room.

We walked down the hall to room three, and as soon as Pate crossed the threshold, she became very distressed. She visualized a horrific scene from sometime in the past; and from her reaction, it was very disturbing.

"There is a man here and he's frantic! He's trying to escape a fire in this room and smoke and fire are beginning to fill the room! Oh, my God! He doesn't make it out, he dies here!" Pate was visibly shaken, and she needed assistance to leave the building.

I was standing there, and as soon as she said fire, I began to think back. The new building we were in was built for Union Square Guest Quarters and had never had a fire. But when we tore down the shell of the old McCroy's Five and Dime store to build the new building, we watched as the demolition crew ripped off the roof with a large crane and exposed the old original timbers dating back to the Arcade Hotel.

I still remember pointing out some charred beams and saying to my wife: *"Look there's been a fire! I guess they put it out before it burned the entire building."*

Charred rafters in the attic—proof of a fire somewhere in the past. Was there a hotel fire somewhere in the past, but one that didn't completely destroy the building? A fire that was confined to the back of the hotel where the Guest Quarters building is now? Did a man die trying to escape, and does his spirit still reside where his old room was in the Arcade hotel? How could Pate have possibly known about a fire in the Arcade Hotel? Is this a coincidence or does Pate have supernatural powers to discern spirits and energy imprints from the past?

I was certain she does after that incident. She made a believer out of me after describing the fire that was in the old Arcade Hotel.

When we left the Union Square Guest Building, we decided to sit in the old Central of Georgia railcar that we had converted into a dining room for the Guest Quarters. When my wife and I were restoring this area of downtown El Dorado, we decided to move in an antique train car to add to the ambience. We found an old Central of Georgia coach car and an El Paso Railway caboose in south-central Texas some 25 years ago and moved them to downtown El Dorado. Over the years, these railcars have been used for a Mexican Restaurant, a Southern bar-b-que restaurant, a Chinese restaurant, and—currently—the breakfast dining car for Guest Quarters.

As soon as we walked in, Pate remarked, *"This palace is full of spirits and imprints."* As a little explanation; Pate says individuals leave an energy imprint when they occupy a place, and she can discern this when she is in a place, and she can actually see the people who have been in those places. These aren't ghosts, but merely flash snapshots of what happened, and she uses this gift to work on modern-day murder and kidnapping cases. (Pate's work with detectives and police departments using this gift has been documented.)

However, as Pate will tell you, in some places actual spirits return to occupy a place that was either attractive to them or a place of great personal tragedy. These are the entities that cause paranormal experiences.

There has been some speculation that the entities have memories that attract them to places, or it could be that they will not leave, or that they come back for tragic reasons. The train car seemed to have thousands of energy imprints and at least one ghost. Pate passed through El Dorado about two years ago and happened to stop by the Guest Quarters to look things over. When she went in the train car, she remarked to our manager that the coach car was teaming with energy imprints, and she could pick up a very strong presence of a spirit.

This was her second time to be in the train car, but evidently the car held some strong memories for her. These were her comments.

"Well the place is clean now, and some of the energies aren't here like they were before, which is a good thing. When I was here before so much was going on that it was hard to pick out the different entities that reside here. When I walked in here the first time, I saw many soldiers and they were Confederate, and these soldiers were in various states—they weren't healthy—looked a little old to be soldiers. Okay? And they were apparently being transported to somewhere, and they had them shoved in kind of like cattle. It was very crowded. It wasn't a comfortable setting for them. They seemed to be going somewhere, but I sure don't think it was to fight in the War, because they weren't armed and they looked too old. I think they are talking about things that happened to them. It sounds as if they are discussing fighting, but in the past."

This is one of the most vivid energy imprints identified by Ms. Tate, and after she left, I reviewed what I knew about the old Central of Georgia coach car. The idea of a car full of unarmed

Confederate soldiers in uniform had me puzzled. However, none of the soldiers were young. In fact many of them looked sick or at least certainly not in any condition to be a part of any conflict, according to Pate.

Confederate soldiers and the coach car didn't seem to go together since the car was built well after the Civil War. However, then I remembered something: The coach car had been built in 1878, 13 years after the War ended, and it went into service for The Central of Georgia Railroad, which was headquartered in Atlanta.

Was this a turn-of-the-century train ride by Confederate veterans heading to Atlanta or Stone Mountain for a reunion? We know the old coach car was in operation in and out of Atlanta during this time and for 50 years after the Civil War was over, and reunions were extremely popular.

Is this another coincidence? No, I think not. Pate's credentials are too impressive to even think that she would invent such a story.

Then Pate nodded as she saw another scene in the train car. It was one of the more interesting and colorful scenes.

"Well, this is really unusual; just a couple of big round heaters at each end of the car and no seats." (When she said that my mouth dropped open. When we bought the car, the holes in the ceiling where the old pot-bellied heaters sat were still there. We covered up the holes and now they are gone without a trace.

"I can see more men again, but the car didn't have any regular train car seats. The car is full of men; no women were in the car. There was a card game going on in the front of the car and several men were on the floor playing a dice game. There was a lot of gambling and some of it was around men playing cards around tables, but some of the gambling was on the floor with dice. These were big, old, rough-looking homemade dice.

"At the other end of the car some men were playing cards, and I have the impression that these were oilmen, because they were dressed rugged and had on work attire and they were arguing about something, and that's when the shooting took place. It was in that corner."

Pate pointed to the northwest corner of the train car.

"Apparently it was over one of the dice games, and a guy got shot right there, literally, with some small-caliber gun. I don't know if it was a derringer; I couldn't tell. It was very fast, very quick."

Pate pointed to the north side of the car, about 8 feet from the corner, where a faint, dark satin was embedded into the wooden floor. *"Evidently, the spirit of the man that was killed is still here, and he is distressed because the man who shot him wasn't arrested. This car full of men didn't seem to be worried about the law, because they ignored the body and just pushed it out of the way and continued the dice game. The man that was shot died, and his ghost is still here!"*

Well, I'll admit I felt a little tingle go up my spine when she said that because I've been in the train car late at night, and I have seen the lights blink and had the hair on the back of my neck stand up.

Then Pate indicated that the scene changed again.

"I see coach seats again and they're full of well dressed men—no women. They are all wearing hats and most of them are smoking cigars. By the way they are dressed, I think this is a scene from the 1920s. There are new seats—much nicer seats—and men sitting in them look like businessmen. They are just traveling, but since the car is packed with men I have the feeling that they're going somewhere to make money or do something that has to do with business."

Was this an oil-boom train full of promoters and speculators who flooded into El Dorado during the early 1920s? Maybe, because the history of the old coach indicates that it was sold and transferred west during this time period, ending up in south Texas.

Did it roll into South Arkansas during the oil boom, when every coach car available was pressed into service?

I stood there in the coach and let my imagination take over for a few seconds. *Pate couldn't have known about the two, black, pot-bellied heaters in each end of the train,* I thought. *We repaired the roof and floor and there was not a trace of them left in the coach car.* As I started to leave the train car there was only one thought in my mind: *This train car is full of ghosts!*

We left the train car and walked a block down the street to the old Rialto Theater, passing the site of the old gallows, where we met a reporter from the "*El Dorado News-Times.*" (I have noted Pate's comments about the plot of ground where the Oil Heritage Park is located in the chapter on the Oil Heritage Park.) A newspaper reporter from the "*El Dorado News-Times,*" Jamie Davis, and a photographer, Jim Lemons, was there to interview Pate. They would accompany her on the first of two visits to the old theater.

17

SPIRITS OF THE RIALTO

PATE entered the Rialto Theater and remarked how cold it was, compared to the air outside. "It's very cold in here," she stated with authority. "That's a good sign for ghosts." (The outside temperature was in the 80s that day.)

Seconds later, she saw the first spirit of the tour—a heavyset man standing on the first landing of the main staircase. "I get the feeling that maybe he owned the place. He sort of takes care of everything, like a caretaker," she said, describing the man as wearing a vest and pocket watch. "Maybe he'll contact us later." (Author's note: The description of this ghost resembles a longtime theater manager known by everyone who attended the Rialto as Mr. Robb. Or it could be Bo Clark, one of the theater owners, according to Ms. Osborne, whose father, Frellsen E. Osborne, operated the theater for approximately 30 years.)

Pate proceeded on her tour to the stage of the main theater, where she saw a second spirit, a young lady dressed in 1920s attire, near the stage. "Her name is Irma," Pate announced.

Later, when Pate returned to the foyer, she noted another spirit, a young boy by the name of Charlie who was running back and forth in the lobby and up the stairs. She had feeling that, "there's been an explosion," she said, leaning against her companion for support. "He lost his daddy. This is where he came to be happy. He wanders through here."

Could this be the explosion that occurred in 1920 when—prior to the first well in Arkansas to encounter hydrocarbons—a well named the # 1 Constantine, hit a gas sand and blew out. It spewed out a huge amount of natural gas, and drew a crowd of people. Tragedy struck when one of the men stuck a match to light a cigarette and ignited a huge explosion that killed several people. Or was this an explosion in one of the early refineries that dotted South Arkansas during the 1920s? Was Charlie's dad one of those people killed at the oil well or at one of the refinery explosions? And was Nora, from room 6 in the Guest Quarters, the wife of the other man who was killed?

There is a side story here. After an article about the Rialto and the ghosts appeared in the Sunday "El Dorado News-Times," I got a call from a lady whose mother spent her last days in Hudson Nursing Home. According to her daughter, Gladys Little, her mother claimed to see many things that Gladys and no one else could see, such as horses passing by the nursing home. And then one day she told her daughter that she had been visited by a young boy named Charlie. Of course, her daughter couldn't see Charlie, but Ms. Little continued to state that Charlie would come by almost daily to see her.

Was this the ghost from the Rialto? Did this elderly lady have psychic powers and actually see Charlie? We'll never know for certain, but, since Hudson Nursing Home is only a few block west of the Rialto, it sure seems reasonable to think that Charlie might have visited someone nearby—someone with psychic powers who could see him and enjoy the benefit of a visit.

After seeing Charlie, Pate sat in the main lobby for a moment to rest—she gets "Woozy," she explained, when she uses her gift. Then she made her way back to the sidewalk where she proclaimed the Rialto, "a very interesting place. It is very busy in there, spirit-wise," she said "This was the center, the absolute center, of entertainment, just the place to be. There are some unbelievable stories here, and I imagine when we get backstage, I'll see a lot of things."

Pate continued the conversation: "Just because there are spirits at the Rialto, it doesn't mean that they are malevolent in nature. People don't understand that all ghosts are human unless they are demons, which are fallen angels. They are, but not always, here out of trauma. A lot of the time, they don't know what to do and get lost, so they go back to places that are familiar to them. They don't know to go into the light," said Pate. "There are definitely some (spirits) here."

We stood in the lobby for another few minutes, while Pate commented about Charlie and the supposed theater manager who was standing on the landing midway up the west flight of stairs. As we walked into the main auditorium, Pate suddenly stopped and focused on the stage. She nodded her head as she approached the stage and began to describe in detail the spirit of the young woman she had earlier noted.

"She's got honey-brown hair, but it's a real light honey-brown; it's curly but it's cut close. I don't know how to express it—kind of like loose curls. And she's got a bow in her hair with ribbon, and the bow is cocked a little bit to the left. She's short, and a dancer of some sort or an entertainer, and she's got a tiny waist but she's kind of plump. She's not real thin. I have the impression from her that she really, really loved dancing here and entertaining here, and I think she was in love with one of the stagehands or could be musician, I'm not sure; but she was in love with somebody, and it didn't get reciprocated.

"I get this feeling of sadness, and it's like she's all happy with the dance, but then there's something that's bothering her, and her feeling goes back into the sadness again. I have a feeling I'll understand more when I get closer."

We walked on down to the stage and Pate pointed to the southwest corner of the stage. "She's right there. Her name is Irma, and she's wearing an outfit with many bright colors, but I don't know how to describe it because I've never seen anything like this. It's not a dress. It is more like a fancy practice outfit. I don't think she's performing; she practicing for something. She's not actively performing. She's practicing. And she's got on these light-colored stockings. Light-colored dance shoes with a strap over them. She's got this really strange, short-type pants that balloon out a little bit, which I thought was really strange. And she's got this dress on that has a lapel that folds this way and one that folds this way and it's kind of like a blouse with a lapel and these puffy sleeves—and she's there and she's acting."

Pate went on to say that she perceived this young lady's emotions jumping from enjoying the dance to feeling deep sorrow. However, she didn't know what her remorse concerned. Evidently, according to Pate, she had been murdered and her spirit had returned to a place where she once found pleasure.

Could this be the young woman dancer who was mysteriously killed late one night after a show? A persistent story has been told of a romance that took place between a prominent town leader, who was married, and a young vaudeville dancer. Because of the distance between them, they rarely saw each other most days. But when the show circuit returned to El Dorado each spring they reconnected.

We walked to the east side of the orchestra pit, and then went down the stairs to below the stage where the old vaudeville dressing rooms were located. We walked into the first room, and Pate shook her head.

"There's a whole bunch of (spirit) people in here, and there were mirrors in here." Pate pointed to the west wall where several holes in the plaster indicated something was fastened to the wall.

There were also, apparently, several ceiling lights together which looked much as if they were used in a dressing room. Pate continued, "Where'd the mirrors go? They should be on that wall there." She pointed to the center of the room's west wall.

"This room is full of a whole lot of busy energy. I'm not just getting one person in particular and it's both male and female. They are coming and going in almost a blur. It's real, real busy (spirit-wise) in here."

We left the dressing room and walked into a large room directly underneath the stage. Pate immediately began to get strong feeling and saw a lot of activity. "I'm getting energy of a physical fight that took place here. Apparently, there were a lot of angry, angry people involved, and I think it started with two men and got a little bit more involved, maybe a couple of others. I'm not sure what the fight's about. But I do know someone was drunk, and I don't know if they were in the orchestra and there was a fight about them being drunk and they got pitched out.

"This was a big confrontation and this person was very, very angry about this, and others involved were very angry also. I don't know why the scene stays here, but it is so vivid that it must have been very dramatic. This may be one of the key events that happened in the theater. The drunken person that was involved was one who repeatedly got drunk."

We left the room beneath the stage and walked up the stairs and behind the curtains to the southwest corner of the stage. Tate immediately began to see men doing various things.

"I guess they're stagehands, and they are sitting around an old table playing cards. I think it's poker, but I'm not sure. This seems to be like a regular thing in-between working gigs. That surprises me. I don't get anything negative. I don't get anything malevolent in this area so far."

We left the stage area, climbed up the east stairwell to the mezzanine, and walked in the ladies rest room. Numerous paranormal sightings have been reported here over the years, and Pate quickly sees the optical aberration.

"Yes, she a very blonde woman, and I don't know why she's here, but she's in a rush to leave, and then she comes back in just as fast. She has on a weird hat with a feather or something on it. I can't quite get it. She's dressed in something very light in color. This looks more like 1930s or '40s because her hair is cut different—low and close to her face. Let me see if I can touch the original doorway, and relate to her. Yes, I'm getting her around the mirror.

"She's always in a rush. I don't think she's a ghost; I think she's an imprint because I can't make contact. I am just getting this rush—a flash as she rushes by. Yes, there's a blonde-haired woman, and she's moving very quickly though. I don't see her. I think she's more of an imprint rather than an actual spirit. I get her moving through hurriedly."

Then Pate walks back out of the lady's rest room, and while she stands there she comments about something:

"That man that I picked up downstairs, I think he runs projection equipment, and I get him coming through here, and he's busy and he's coming and going in through here now, he wasn't so much downstairs, but he is now."

Pate goes to the part of the balcony where, when the theater was segregated, the black patrons sat.

"I see a lot of people around here. There are blacks all dressed up to come to the theater. I don't know what this is—maybe a ghost, or an energy imprint—but I'm getting a black woman wearing a red dress. She's heavy and she's wearing a red, low-cut dress—heavy-set, not like three hundred pounds or anything, but she's a big woman, big bust. I can't tell what she's about." (Author's note: Pate could not have known she was in the formerly segregated part of the balcony. All the separating rails and even the seats had been replaced.)

Pate went into the original projection room and immediately began to visualize something.

"What's going on in here? Oh, there's lots of smoking in here. This is that guy's domain. This is his domain. He owns this. This is his. He doesn't like people in here at all. He's the old projectionist. He's got gray hair. I can't tell exactly because he's got a cap on and the cap looks grayish or light tan. It's a flat cap with a little rim. I suspect his hair is thinning, but I can't tell for sure. He's medium-build, but strong. Although I think as he got older he lost a lot of weight. I'm sure people have had to have seen him because he was here so long. "He's got kind of a plain face. I think he's got a mustache, and he has on some very weird pants. I don't know what they're called, but they look corrugated or ribbed. I don't know what the material is, but I'm sure there's a name for the material. Maybe he's the owner or the manager. Yes, he seems to be there. But the one that's really, really active is the one in the projection room. He's all over the place, he's not just there. Because he's also like the handyman. I get the impression like this is his home, literally. He might have even slept here."

Pate left the projection room and walked to the main west staircase where she described the same man she saw earlier in the day, standing at the same place, on the stairwell landing.

"He's got on a coat/vest/pants. I don't really know how old he is. He's got a bit of a belly to him. He's not real tall or anything. He's another one that smokes a cigar, and has a mustache and kind of thinning hair. I get the feeling he's got some sort of vested interest in the theater. Wants to make sure everything's okay." (Author's note: That is a perfect description of the former theater manager, Mr. Robb. And the smell of cigar smoke is one of the most common of the paranormal experiences reported in the theater.)

Pate's seemed drained of energy, so we left the theater and went outside where she sat on one of the benches and rested.

18

SPIRIT SEEKERS

The Spirit Seekers of Arkansas investigation: March 15, 2008

Final ReportInvestigation Number 03152008

Rialto Theater El Dorado, Arkansas

Number of 35 mm picture taken: 0; Number of digital photos taken: 1027: Minutes of Audio used: 14: Minutes of Video taken: 224 minutes: Number of Positive Photos: 6 digital and 2 on video: Number of EVP recorded: 2

Phenomena captured on film: (Comments from the lead investigator.) This investigation was a very special one in that it presented several obstacles for us to overcome. I put together a handpicked team of investigators each picked for a special talent that they could bring to the investigation. The first obstacle was the size of the building. It has four floors of space that is packed full of small nooks and hidden rooms. The next item to take into consideration is that it is very old and one of the crown jewels of the historic district of El Dorado.

Another opportunity to take into consideration was that it would be very high profile and all of El Dorado would be watching. Last but most definitely not least was that an all night band had been scheduled to play across the street for a downtown party. We overcame these obstacles with the help of a great Spirit Seekers team of investigators. Even with all of the obstacles presented, we managed to find some scientific signs of a haunting. We photographed some orbs of interest. Some were in motion and some were at rest. We found that the air was full of dust inside the old theater but that if a person sat down and was still for a while the dust would settle and the real energy orbs would come around to see what we were doing. To be an energy orb they must be very close to round in shape, dense in nature and show motion. We did capture some of these types of orbs. Some of the activity was captured on video as well. Three different cameras at three different locations caught orbs in motion.

The bulk of the evidence gathered was found around the stage. I had to wait till late in the morning to attempt to gather EVP (electronic voice phenomenon). I was somewhat successful. The EVP captured was in the dressing room under the stage and in the back rows of the seating on the lower level.

Summation: Due to the fact that investigation was very special and I had lots of area to cover, we used a medium size group of investigators. A group of ten investigators were used on this investigation. The team psychic (Angela) was inserted in to the theater at 7 pm with an investigator in training (Natalie). They were allowed to do their walk through independently while the others set up equipment and I interviewed the owner. Upon completion of Angela's psychic evaluation, they were extracted to be interviewed by me individually. While they were being interviewed the others went around the theater taking pictures and various climatic readings. During the interview Angela revealed that first and foremost the theater is full of residual energy. She felt that there were four active spirits in the theater and that they were very curious. She had no encounter with negative energy of any kind. Angela felt the presence of an actress in the dressing room below stage. She said that the actress was hanging around because this is where she belonged. A page played peek-a-boo with her in front of the stage. A group of teens were in the back hanging around waiting as if their group was incomplete. She ran into an elderly worker in the upstairs control room. He was still there because he had nowhere else to go. Some of the group had personal encounters. One felt as if she had been grabbed by the ankle. Another smelt perfume in the upstairs lobby. Several of the group had their batteries drained prematurely. One of the investigators felt as if she was being followed. We saw a door open slightly in the area under the stage. When we tried to make it do it again we found that the door felt like it was dragging the floor and was very hard to move. (Authors note: The identical paranormal experience was reported by Kristin Pope.)

Conclusion: According to the client, focus of the supernatural activity is not centered in any one room but rather dispersed throughout the theater. We at Spirit Seekers believe this to be a true assessment of the haunting also because the amount of evidence gathered during this investigation was taken in just about every corner of the theater.

Is the Rialto Theater in El Dorado, Arkansas haunted? We have a grading system that helps us to answer such questions. We graded the evidence as follows; scientific evidence is photos, video, EMF readings, Temperature readings and EVP. On a scale of 0 – 50 we gave the scientific evidence gathered a 38. The evidence was there and it was fairly strong. Sensory evidence is that of the human five senses and on a scale of 0 – 25 we gave the sensory evidence a 20 because of the fact that so many of the investigators had experiences and some of them were of the same nature and same location at different times. The extra sensory evidence is the feelings of the psychic and sensitive. On a scale of 0 – 25 we gave the extra sensory evidence a 22. In this case the psychic evidence is rated so high because of the fact that another psychic had made a visit to the Rialto one week prior to our visit. Considering an independent viewing of the psychic impressions, I saw an amazing similarity between the two. They were so close to seeing or feeling the same things in the same locations that it would be hard to not use it as evidence. The grand total for this project is 80. The grading system of all evidence gathered tells us that there is a strong possibility that there is paranormal activity happening in the dark recesses of the Rialto Theater in El Dorado.

Investigators signature:

A LOWE

....

Investigation by the Louisiana Spirits
The Rialto Theater, El Dorado, Arkansas

History:

The McWilliams family built the original Rialto Theater in the spring of 1921. They did extensive remodeling in the fall of 1925, and in 1928, the original theater was demolished and the current theater was constructed on the same site. The new Rialto Theater opened in September of 1929. It boasted the latest in acoustical technology for its era and was one of the most modern theaters in the Southwest. The new building seated 1,400 people on the main floor and two balconies. The Rialto closed from 1983 until December of 1987 when it was reopened after extensive remodeling. The Rialto is currently owned by Richard and Vertis Mason and is, again, closed for remodeling.

Reported Activity:

The reports of activity at the Rialto are many. People have smelled scents of perfume, heard footsteps, and strange noises, and odd lights and shadows have been seen. Some say in the balcony area a man has been seen climbing the stairs to the projection booth.

Investigation:

Louisiana Spirits arrived at the Rialto on October 11, 2008 to begin our investigation. In preparation, we set up 8 IR cameras and two DVD recorders. The investigators were each equipped with their personal EMF detectors, digital cameras, audio recorders, one Sony Night Shot Camcorder and one Flir Thermal Imaging camera. Our group of six divided into groups of two and we began our investigation. There were quite a few personal experiences that night. Two investigators on the stage were trying to get a response from whatever paranormal entity may be occupying the place and they said it sounded as if someone started running up and down the catwalk overhead. (Author's note: I have heard the footsteps on the catwalk—my report is in the last chapter of the book.) The noises were caught on audio and the reaction to this was recorded on video.

Another group of investigators heard what sounded to be like a loud hiss or shushing noise in the auditorium, which could not be explained. One investigator heard someone repeat "O.K." after she had said it. It came from directly behind her, but there was only her and another investigator in the room at the time and he was in front of her and had not said anything at that time. An investigator decided to tap out a little tune on the stage to see if someone or something would finish it and several seconds afterwards, he got what he asked for. There was a light "knock knock" shortly thereafter. Several investigators, while seated on the stage, saw "little green lights" flashing in the auditorium area. They were literally from the ceiling to the floor and all areas in between, resembling fireflies. We were able to capture some audio; however, due to the loud music outside of the theater, we are unable to use most of it. We do, however, look forward to returning to the Rialto in the very near future for a follow-up investigation, and hopefully it will be quieter.

I have attached the write up regarding the investigation of the Rialto, as well as some of the evidence that we found. The video clip could just be a spider web or something, but it was interesting anyway. Also, you may need headphones to listen to the evps. The picture is a bright orb that was taken in the main auditorium. As you can see, it is up towards the ceiling and there are no light bulbs in that area. If you have any questions, please feel free to ask! We are so looking forward to returning there in January. Thank you for allowing us the opportunity to investigate such a fabulous place! If you would like to view our website and the write up, you can check it out at www.laspirits.com Just click the "investigations" tab and then the "historical locations" tab and scroll to the bottom, then click the Rialto Theater.

Again, we thank you for allowing us in your theater and we look forward to our return visit.

Sincerely, Rachael Ellis, Louisiana Spirits

Investigation Report
The Rialto Theater, El Dorado Arkansas

Mr. Mason

First I would like to thank you for letting us visit and investigate The Rialto Theater. It was a great investigation. Mrs. Graves was so nice to us. Please thank her for us for taking time out of her weekend to show us around. We also got to meet her family, her kids are so sweet. Also Mr. Givens was so helpful to us. Please thank him for us for all the phone calls.

REPORT

We came in and set up 7 IR cams throughout the theater. We also had 5 digital cameras-5 hand video IR cameras, 6 EMF meters and 10 digital voice recorders, all placed throughout the building. We started our investigation about 6:30 pm. Three investigators went up to the 2nd and 3rd floors, and 2 were in the theater and switched out throughout the night. We did pick up lots of bangs, and different noises throughout the night, and 2 of our investigators did have a personal experience.

EVP: Electronic Voice Phenomena: An EVP is a disembodied voice that is recorded by electronic methods. These methods can include a voice recorder or even by the audio of a video camera. To capture EVP's our investigators ask a series of questions, with a brief bit of silence between questions. While nothing can be heard by the ear at the time, when you play back the recording you may hear voices that may answer the questions.

EMF: Electromagnetic Field Detector: This is known as an EMF detector. It is used during investigations to locate electromagnetic fields in suspected paranormal activity spots. Ghost/Spirits have been known to produce this energy while manifesting themselves.

Orbs: There are several different kinds of orbs. There are water spot orbs. Most come from dew outside. There are dust orbs, just particles of dust in the air. Every building has them. They are very common. Then there are energy orbs. Any place with electricity will have them. In theory, ghost or spirits will try to use the energy in them to try and manifest themselves. This energy orb will pull away and have its own path different from the air flow. Also can be different colors, as in Pink-green-orange-purple or blue. This does not mean you have ghost or spirits. This just means you have an environment change with enough energy in it for an orb to form. But it also means you have a better chance of a spirit manifesting itself if you were to have one.

While sitting on the stage, we were asking questions and we did get an EVF spike. And with the time stamp on the voice recorder, we did pick up an EVP; also the temp did change, but only in one spot, so therefore we did get an evp-emf spot in a time frame. This is a good indication of spirit activity.

While 3 investigators were on the second floor all 3 picked up a strange smell and could not find where it was coming from. The smell went away as quick as it came. They compared it to cigar smoke.

EVP: #1. Sounds like man, think it says (you don't belong down-here get out) EVP#2. Sounds like a girl, faint whisper (I don't like you)

Cam. # 1 was set in the basement. Cam # 2 was set stage left. Cam # 3 was a theater setting (right side) Cam # 4, backup to cam # 3. Cam # 5, theater 2nd floor. Cam # 6 in front of the theater on the right. Cam # 7 box office or ticket booth. Cam # 8 piano room 2nd floor.

Reports: Cam # 5 dust orb. Cam # 3 dust orb. Cam # 5 dust orb. Cam # 6 dust orb. Cam # 6 dust orb. Cam # 6 dust orb. Cam # 7 dust orb. Cam # 6 dust orb. At 10:03 all on Cam 6—3 different electric orbs east with its own path, not going the way of the air flow. 10:12 Cam # 3 This energy orb came from over the top of Cam # 3 bounced from 4th row setting to the second row.

The Rialto Project—Ghost Hunting

Some of the most vivid encounters occurred when a group of college students spent several hours late one night in the theater. This project was undertaken by six college students using very sensitive recording devices and infrared cameras. The team members were Rachelle Moore, Kristi Covington, Jeff McKinney, Jennifer Horn, Keely McKinney, and Thomas Hart. They spent most of their time in the upstairs area where the theater restrooms are located. Of all the areas in the Rialto, this one is probably cited as the most active place for paranormal activity.

A young blonde woman has been seen by numerous individuals, and the psychic, Carol Tate describes her as "very blonde, and in a big hurry to get somewhere. She is continually coming in and out of the ladies' rest room."

The following audio sounds were recorded by the investigating team:

Upstairs theater: "Dance"

Lobby: "Ask me."; Lobby: "Don't talk."

Upstairs bathroom: "Run fast—run."; "Row your boat."; "Can't catch me."; laughter; "Home."; "I… Keely, bring Jennifer."; "I want to play."; "I want you to stay."; "I want to play or stay."; "I want you to stay."

In addition to the audio, <u>several remarkable photos show ghostly apparitions</u>.

19

THE RANDOLPH AND GARRETT HOTELS

THE stories of ghosts, legends, and scoundrels in downtown El Dorado wouldn't be complete without delving into the checkered history of the city's former premier hotels, the Randolph and the Garrett. Both of these hotels were on South Washington Avenue, a block from the Rialto Theater. These long-since vanished hotels were the two Grande Dames of the city. The Garrett was constructed in 1908 and the Randolph in the mid 1920s. In every account of El Dorado's vivid oil-boom history, these two hotels are prominently featured.

The most celebrated of the hotels was the Garrett, whose lobby was the epicenter of oil-leasing and deal-making activity during the early years of the boom. In the lobby of the hotel, lease hounds and speculators made a market for stock in the hundreds of small oil companies that were drilling wells in South Arkansas. Most of these companies were operating as open-ended trusts, which allowed them to sell unlimited amounts of stock in each well they drilled.

An open-ended trust is a simple way to steal money from investors. It's illegal today, and it was illegal then. However, enforcement of security laws in the boomtowns of Arkansas and Texas was almost nonexistent, as was the enforcement of nationwide prohibition during that time.

The reason an open-ended trust is illegal is very simple: If you, as an investor, purchase stock in one of these companies, the other stockholders immediately have the value of their stock diluted. In other words there was no limit to the amount of stock that a promoter would, or could, sell.

However, if you happened to buy stock in one of the companies that completed one of the huge wells in the Smackover Field, you received a dividend based on the number of shares you owned. And many times the cash flow was so large that the oil operators were able to pay enormous dividends and the investors forgot about their stock being diluted.

Naturally, when a well was drilling,—owned by an operator's trust—the rumors of success could send the stock of the trust skyrocketing. And since money and greed were always present, the temptation to lie and cheat the unwary investor was great. Of course, a gusher would guarantee immediate riches for an investor, but a dry hole would cause the value of their investment to plunge to zero. It was a gambler's game and, to hedge the odds, slick traders used inside, usually unreliable information and rumors of big strikes, skinning the new investors who showed up.

In the 1920s, these two hotels were the best accommodations available, but even with more than 100 rooms in each hotel, they could not accommodate the large numbers of people looking for a place to stay. Both hotels were packed every night, and cots were set up in the lobbies and back reception rooms to accommodate the overflow of people.

But that wasn't enough, and immediately west of South Washington Avenue a huge tent city sprouted up overnight. Hundreds of tents filled the open fields and a bed for the night could be rented for $1. Of course, it was a cot and blanket, and you shared a tent with as many as 20 men. It was around the edge of this tent city and in the alleyways behind the hotels that hijackers stalked their prey. And a few steps away from this tent city along South Washington Avenue, these gangs lurked in alleyways—and hundreds of men met their death.

***

The Randolph Hotel, while almost as grand as the Garrett, attracted a different crowd, and soon after it opened rumors of the "Girls of the Randolph" were something that even schoolboys throughout the county knew about. As a student at Norphlet High School during the 1950s, I was not only aware of the "Girls," I heard countless stories about how they were part of a circuit of prostitutes who traveled from Hot Springs, Shreveport, El Dorado and even down to Jackson, Miss.. It never occurred to me why the State Police, the Union County Sheriff's Office or the El Dorado City Police Department didn't stop the prostitution. It would have been virtually impossible for law enforcement officials not to be aware of what was going on.

Another hotel, not as well known, was simply called Mrs. Smith's Hotel. It was located on the corner of Cedar Street and South Washington Avenue: a big wooden structure with four floors, built to handle the more common workers of the oil-boom crowds. Evidently, it was a rather rough place considering the accounts of men thrown out the upstairs windows late at night.

Just walking by the hotel on the sidewalk was so dangerous that after dark folks walked out into Cedar Street for safety, according to an eyewitness. While Mrs. Smith's Hotel didn't have the glamour of the other nearby hotels, it was home to many of the most colorful characters that swept into the city after the discovery of oil.

During the oil boom of the 1920s, the city seemed to shift its center, from the downtown around the Courthouse Square, to the area around the theater and the area one block east to where South Washington Street began its "descent into hell," as one old-timer called it.

South Washington Avenue, one of El Dorado's major north-south avenues, extends south past the courthouse, and then as it passes the site of the old Garrett Hotel, (now BancorpSouth), it begins a gradual descent until it intersects with Hillsboro Street approximately a half-mile away. The portion of the street between BancorpSouth and Hillsboro Street was called Hamburger Row during the first two years of the 1920s oil boom. The city council had authorized sidewalk hamburger stands because of the lack of restaurants.

My "Girls of the Randolph" story

"Don't call it a whorehouse," Momma whispered, shaking her finger at me. I was 15 and a sophomore at Norphlet High School when a senior filled me in on the details. Of course, I'd heard comments about "The Girls of the Randolph" years before, but I'd just thought my friends were making things up.

Well, they weren't. And when I came home and asked mother about the girls and mentioned "whorehouse" she went into that defensive "Don't talk—don't tell" mode that residents of South Arkansas have taken for years: Yep, sweep it under the rug—and for sure, don't mention it in public.

But it's a fact that prostitutes were available at many locations, starting at the beginning of the oil boom of the 1920s, until well into the 1970s. Of course, since it was common knowledge to schoolboys from small towns in the area, you can be sure that all of the law enforcement officers, elected officials, and businessmen in the county knew about the "girls."

Mother leaned over and said very softly, "Those ladies that stay there may be just temporary help for the hotel."

Well, I smiled and just went back to whatever I was doing. My mom was part of the cover-up. The "Girls of the Randolph" who were working prostitutes, had been an El Dorado fixture as long as anyone can remember.

During the 1940s and '50s there was a Magnolia Petroleum Service Station across the street from the Rialto Theater, and, as a young girl, Mrs. Bill (Dot) Craig helped her father, who owned the station. She tells the following story about "The Girls of the Randolph."

"I remember working at the station that day, and about mid-morning a very attractive, well dressed lady in a big sedan pulled up and wanted her car filled up, washed, and the oil changed. While we were working on her car she got out and went in the office and talked with my mother, who kept books for the station. I remember hearing them laughing and talking and the lady stayed and talked with Mother even after we finished with her car.

"Well, the lady finally left with goodbyes to all and after she drove off I went in the office where mother had leaned back in her chair and had lit a cigarette. When I inquired about the 'nice lady,' Mother smiled and said, 'I never met a whore I didn't like.'

"Of course, I'd heard talk about the 'Girls of the Randolph' but I'd never even considered that my mother would know anything about them, or that she would actually use the word 'whore.' I know I must have looked shocked, because she said, 'Oh, that was the madam. She on her way to Vicksburg to swap out the girls.'"

Recently a lady from El Dorado, who will remain nameless, told me the following story about the Randolph Hotel. She was a college student during the late 1940s and during the summer between her junior and senior years, she got a job working for one of the largest companies in El Dorado. She worked downtown, and during that summer, she got a first-hand glimpse of the hotel activities.

"After a few weeks my boss, who was married and one of the leading businessmen of the town, went around our office and invited several secretaries, including me, to join him and his friends that afternoon after work for a drink at the Petroleum Club."

The Petroleum Club was located on the second floor of the Randolph Hotel and patrons entered through the back door of the hotel. One of the members and frequent visitors to the Club told me that during the 1940s and '50s, it was the only place in town where you could buy a mixed drink. According to this now retired businessman, the Petroleum Club had a long bar across the back wall and tables and chairs filled the large room. It was frequently used as a meeting place for fraternal organizations.

"Of course we were flattered and excited about being invited to join a group of men in a place that had a reputation like the Randolph Hotel. I don't think I would have gone if several of the other girls hadn't gone with me. That afternoon started what would become a regular 'Meet us at the Petroleum Club' outing, and we had drinks with a group of prominent El Dorado businessmen at least once a week, usually on Friday afternoons.

"The meeting for drinks with our group of secretaries and businessmen had several unusual twists. Even though our office closed exactly at 5 o'clock and our boss was always there right up to quitting time, he never accompanied us on the two-block walk down the street to the Hotel. He would always have to do something else, and told us he would meet us there. Of course, we were young, naive girls and it wasn't until later that I realized he didn't want to be seen walking right through the center of town and going in the back of the hotel with three to five attractive young girls.

"The other unusual part of the meeting for drinks was what we called 'Time.' When we walked up the stairs to the Club, we were met by sometimes as many as 10 businessmen who would welcome us and sometimes those warm welcomes would be accompanied by a rather overly affectionate hugs and squeezes. Then we would be asked what we would like to drink, and, of course, the idea of flirting with a group of older men, smoking and drinking mixed drinks had us twittering. Several of us were certainly under the age of 21, but at the Petroleum Club no one ever asked us for an I. D. I don't have any idea if the Club had a license to sell mixed drinks, but I do know it was the only place in town that you could order one.

"After we finished our drinks our boss would usher us to the door with an admonition, 'I know you girls need to be getting home.' Of course, the men didn't leave, and we speculated many times about what went on after we left. I don't know if any of those flirtations ever went any further than just what we did when we were at the Petroleum Club, but I will tell you this: Some of the girls went a lot further than others. As far as I was concerned it was just a lark to go there and do something that we thought of as forbidden, and as for me that was all it was."

I asked if she had ever seen any of the "Girls of the Randolph" in the Petroleum Club.

"No, I never did, but since we were ushered out at about 6:30 it was probably before those girls went to work."

She laughed; then seemed to remember something and said:

"But you know something? One night after a movie at the Majestic Theater, which was next door to the Randolph, I saw one of those businessmen arm-in-arm with what I am sure was one of those girls. She had on more makeup than any decent girl would ever put on. I watched them until they walked into the hotel. Of course, I thought that was very interesting and when I got home I told my mother about it. I was shocked at what she said: 'Don't ever let me hear you repeat what you told me, and whatever you do don't tell anyone else.'

"That surprised me, but, thinking back on it, I guess that's the way things were in El Dorado during the '40s and '50s. Everybody knew about the "Girls of the Randolph," including the local police, the mayor, the sheriff, and church leaders, but evidently the men who the girls accommodated had enough political pull to keep the prostitutes in business, despite the fact that everyone in the county knew what was going on."

However, all the "girls" weren't at the Randolph or in the small hotels that lined South Washington Avenue and Cedar Street. Here is an account about those "ladies of the night," or you might say "ladies of the late afternoon," operating on Main Street almost across from First Baptist Church.

From an unnamed source:

"In the mid-1950s, we had offices in what was known as the First National Bank Tower. Our west windows looked directly into a hotel—which I can't remember the name of. It was where the present Chamber of Commerce is now located, and was also the site of a

Sterling's Department Store on the ground floor. We had only been there a few days when we realized there were prostitutes living in the upper floors of the hotel. Every day, sometime around 5 o'clock, the girls would entertain visitors, and never pulled down the window shades. It became such a show that quite a crowd would gather at our office every afternoon for drinks and to watch the show. It was something to see."

Prostitutes working on Main Street across from First Baptist Church during the 1950s seemed to be just part of what the residue left by the oil boom in El Dorado. As far as I know, none of the girls were ever prosecuted or even charged; the good, church-going folks from First Baptist just looked the other way, as did everyone else in town.

Another account comes from a current executive whose stay in the Garrett Hotel, across the street from the Randolph Hotel, accorded him a bird's-eye view of the nighttime activities that were occurring in the Randolph. This is his story.

"My father came to El Dorado in the late 1940 to manage a family business, and I accompanied him on several of his trips. I was probably twelve or thirteen years old, and I relished coming to El Dorado because of all the excitement that was still left over from the 1920s oil boom. We stayed at the Garrett Hotel and my room was on the third floor. The windows in my room overlooked Cedar Street.

"The main entrance to the Randolph Hotel was through two big double doors facing South Washington Street, but there were two additional entrances: one on Cedar Street and the other at the rear of the building. The rear entrance was the entrance to the Petroleum

Club. The Cedar Street entrance was a secondary, more discrete, entrance and allowed someone from the street to enter the hotel and go directly to the upstairs rooms without making a grand entrance via the big, double doors on Washington Street and walking across a vast lobby.

"Well, after I'd been in the Garrett Hotel for a few days I realized my window faced the third floor windows of the Randolph. Furthermore, as I peered out my window, I noted the row of rooms across from me had Venetian blinds for shades and even though they were down on most of the windows, I could see through the only partially closed slats. What I saw, as night after night I stayed glued to my seat in the window, shocked me to no end. I witnessed first-hand the "Girls of the Randolph" practicing their trade.

"Of course, from that vantage point I could look down and see their customers as they went in through the side door of the hotel, and since there was a streetlight nearby and the sidelights to the door were always on, I could see many of the customers. There were many that I didn't recognize, but the ones I did recognize surprised me. I won't call their names, but I can assure you they were some of the most prominent businessmen in El Dorado."

(Author's note: I tried to pry out the names for months, but the gentleman who gave me the interview would only say that some of the men he recognized were leading citizens of the community.)

Another item of interest concerning the "Girls of the Randolph" comes from a former judge in Union County, who added this bit of information.

"The girls were prostitutes who traveled the Arkansas circuit from Texarkana to Hot Springs to El Dorado. I don't know how many girls were on the circuit, but evidently it was several dozen."

Of course, during the oil boom of the 1920s, South Washington Avenue and other nearby streets were lined with barrelhouses and both large and small hotels that offered girls along with their rooms. South Washington Avenue, or Hamburger Row as it was called in the early 1920s, was lined with them. However, instead of disappearing after the oil boom, many of them lasted up until the late 1950s. They posed as small hotels, as opposed to wide-open saloons. An eyewitness, who was a desk clerk at the Garrett Hotel, gave me this account.

"Sure, everybody knew about the girls at the Randolph Hotel. But the Garrett Hotel, where I worked, didn't allow that. I remember a number of soldiers returning from the War coming by the Garrett and asking about the girls. Well, we didn't have girls at the Garrett, but they were right across the street, and not only there, in the Randolph, but there were two other hotels on down South Washington Street with girls, and believe it or not, in the two blocks between the Garrett Hotel and First Methodist Church there were three small hotels that had prostitutes. It was easy to spot these bordellos, because of the male traffic that entered and left after being there for not more than an hour."

Well, the Randolph Hotel and the other five hotels are gone now, but considering the eyewitness from the vantage point of the Garrett Hotel lobby in 1953, it's shocking to think that six whorehouses were within a block of the Rialto Theater.

My source tells another story that will bring smiles to some of the older citizens of El Dorado. I'm sure this account, from the same man who recounted the viewing via an upstairs room at the Garrett as a 13-year-old boy, will ring some memory bells.

> "There was a very prominent doctor-turned-oilman in town who had a brother that was almost the very opposite of the respected doctor. He had a special way to visit the prostitutes at the Randolph. I would look out the window from the Garrett and watch a long limo drive up to the side entrance to the hotel. And out of that limo would stroll the doctor's brother. He would enter the side door of the hotel and be gone around an hour while his driver stayed double-parked in the street outside the side door of the hotel. Cedar Street was one of the busiest streets in town, and naturally, the double-parked limo created havoc with traffic. But of course, the police ignored the traffic violation. They weren't about to arrest a respected doctor's brother for visiting a prostitute."

That was 1953, and open prostitution at the Randolph and several other small hotels was well known in South Arkansas. Why didn't law enforcement shut them down? Well, I guess we need to look at Hot Springs, Arkansas, during the 1950s.

Along Central Avenue, in the center of Hot Springs, gambling casinos run by the New York mob—and wide-open prostitution—were prevalent. The attorney general of Arkansas was spotted numerous times visiting what were called "clubs" along Central Avenue. When Gov. Faubus was asked about the situation he said, "I don't know anything about it. If someone will bring me proof that gambling is going on down there, I'll shut them down."

Naturally, it was hard for the governor to say that with a straight face, since the whole state knew about the gambling and prostitution going on in Hot Springs. Of course, Gov. Faubus never did do anything about the gambling in Hot Springs, and to think the governor of the state feigned ignorance is hard to believe, but that was just the way things were in the 1950s. It seems El Dorado was in very much the same situation because almost everyone in town knew about the prostitutes—including the mayor, city council, and the police. But the bordellos continued to operate for years.

I have added the stories about the "Girls of the Randolph" because several of the most persistent stories about seeing spirits in the Rialto Theater has to do with one of the girls from the Randolph Hotel. The stories seem to have come from the late 1920s, and I've heard several variations, but the most repeated one has to do with a prominent businessman's continuing affair with one of the prostitutes who lived in the Randolph Hotel.

It seems, according to the rumored story, that a local businessman became enamored with a very special call girl, and he never missed seeing her when she came to town. As the affair continued, he convinced her—with consent of the hotel management—to not travel the circuit with the other girls. He wanted her to stay as a permanent resident of the hotel, where they could be together as much as he desired.

That arrangement seemed to work fine for a few months, but as is the case with most mistresses, she wanted more than to just stay in a hotel room and be available when a man wanted to be with her. She wanted to go out and see movies, have a drink at the Petroleum Club, and maybe do some shopping. The call girl finally convinced her boyfriend to at least take her to an occasional movie, so they would catch the late show at the Rialto, always sitting in the balcony. As the story goes, the young woman became more demanding about going out, and the businessman began to worry more and more about being seen with her. The climax to their relationship came late one night in that very balcony.

Based on legends and various other accounts, the couple's meeting that night went something like this fictional account.

"Oh, I wish we didn't have to sneak up here in the balcony when we go out. Why can't we go to some place nice for dinner some night?"

"You know why. El Dorado gossips would have us spread all over town by the next day."

"Well, you told me if your wife knew about me, it wouldn't surprise her."

"You don't understand how things are in this town. It's one thing for us to do this in the shadows, but not out in front of everybody. The sheriff, mayor, and the city council probably all know about us, and the police sure do—that's the way this town works; But if I took you to a public place, there'd be several men who would come talk to me."

"Why don't you ask your wife for a divorce? Then, after the divorce, we could see each other and, later, get married."

"Naw, I can't do that. It'd be bad for business. We've gotta keep doing exactly what we're doing right now."

"I don't know if I can keep this up, and, well, there's something else... I'm pregnant."

"What? I thought you girls took care of that kind of thing!"

"Oh, we do, but I stopped doing anything because I want to have your baby."

"You can't do that! It would ruin me! Listen to me, girl, you do something to get rid of that baby. Anything!"

"No!"

"What do you mean, 'No'?"

"I'm having this baby, and then we can work out how you'll take care of me and the baby, and later, after your divorce, we can get married. I've thought it all out and that's what we're going to do."

"Oh, for God's sake! Surely you're not serious!"

"Yes, I am, and I'm not changing my mind!"

Evidently, the conversation became more and more heated until the two left the theater shouting at each other. The last thing anyone heard was the girl say,

"We'll meet here tomorrow and finish this; you can tell me your decision."

No one knows what went on that next night, but the story of happened might have something to do with the theater's cleaning crew, which had just begun cleaning the balcony late that night they came upon a grisly sight. The young woman was lying behind the last row of seats in the balcony—dead—with her throat cut.

Is the persistent ghost that haunts the girls' rest room and the balcony the spirit of the young woman who was murdered in the balcony? Psychic Carol Pate contends there is a blonde lady rushing in and out of the ladies' rest room, seemingly in a hurry to go somewhere. She seems to be in distress. This could be the murdered prostitute's ghost looking for her killer, who was never apprehended. (Author's note: A notorious blonde prostitute in El Dorado worked at several brothels on South Washington Avenue. According to what I have pieced together, she began as a prostitute and later became a madam. She worked at The Crystal Hotel as well as several other bordellos along the street. The woman was called "Blondie" at The Crystal Hotel, and she is possibly the same notorious prostitute who picked up the nickname "Two-Shot Blondie."

Was she murdered in the balcony of the Rialto Theater, and does the spirit of Blondie haunt the Rialto ladies' room today? Maybe.

20

THE CRYSTAL HOTEL AND...BORDELLO

IN 1922, after the initial excitement of the oil boom wore off and the town saw the boom wasn't going to be a flash in the pan, several businessmen began working to build more substantial buildings on South Washington Avenue, old Hamburger Row.

This was the 1922-24 version of urban renewal, since almost all of the first makeshift wooden buildings were leveled. Local businessmen were eager to build more substantial structures, and with the flood of oil money flowing into town a mini building boom swept down South Washington Avenue.

Pete McCall, a former Arkansas lieutenant governor, constructed several buildings using convict labor. In fact, his convict labor crews built two of the earliest brick buildings across from the old Presbyterian Cemetery on the south end of Washington Avenue. He completed the first two-story brick building in 1922 and the second, two years later, in 1924. Both buildings had restaurants and assorted retail stores on the first floor, as well as rooms to rent on the second.

The second building was named *The Crystal Hotel*.

The McCall buildings were very similar to other structures that were quickly constructed up and down South Washington Avenue. They each had either restaurants or some semblance of retail on the ground floor, along with a separate entrance that went to the second floor. These second-floor hotels or "rooms" as they were called in an early City Directory, were actually bordellos.

The Crystal Hotel immediately began to serve its customers shortly after the building was completed, and the hotel stayed in business until 1974. Without a doubt, The Crystal Hotel, which was a bordello for 50 years, holds the record for the longest continually operating bordello in the state, and probably one of the longest in the nation.

From interviews and comments made by the present owner of the building, and repetitious conversations from fathers and grandfathers, I have been able to piece together a lot of information about this old, haunted bordello. Yes, the building is haunted, and only the Rialto surpasses it in tales of paranormal activities.

First, let's take a look at how The Crystal Hotel appeared in its heyday during the '20s, '30s, and '40s.

After climbing the stairs to the second floor of the building, a patron would step out into a large, tastefully decorated room. It was a reception area for customers, complete with a red upholstered (with nail-heads) piano and full bar. A rather large, imposing man would meet you. He was the bouncer. If you passed muster, he let you pass, and then a gorgeous red-haired woman—the legendary, lesbian madam of Hamburger Row, Miss Betty Fortenberry—greeted you. Evidently, Betty owned and frequented several of the numerous bordellos on South Washington Avenue, and she stayed at different ones almost nightly. She had her own room at The Crystal Hotel.

Drinks were on the house, if you were a paying customer and hadn't just walked up the stairs to look. Of course, cards and dice were available for any interested patrons. (Yes, it was during Prohibition and gambling and prostitution were illegal, but this was the oil boomtown of El Dorado in the 1920s.)

Girls would be stationed around the room, and as the piano played and the whiskey flowed, they mingled with the customers.

If an invitation to visit one of the girls in her room was accepted, the madam made sure the proper payment was made prior to a man leaving with her.

There are numerous handed-down stories about the girls, the bouncer, and, of course, the madam. One of the more popular girls I've mentioned went by the nickname "Blondie." I'm not sure if this Blondie is the same girl who later became a noted madam, "Two-Shot Blondie" in one of the other bordellos. We do know after being in the bordello for a number of years she quit and became a taxi dispatcher. The cab company she worked for operated for a number of years next door to The Crystal Hotel.

Lee Ann Herndon, the present owner of the building, told me several fascinating stories about its history. Today the building houses *Oddities, Novelties & More* on the first floor, and the second floor has been converted into apartments. One of the more interesting stories was told to Lee Ann by her grandfather.

It seems, that right after the Second World War, Lee Ann's grandfather and six other Marines decided to visit The Crystal Hotel bordello. They marched up the stairs, with its red light in the stairwell, and at the top of the stairs, the house bouncer met them.

"Boys, y'all are welcome, but please don't be rowdy or cause any trouble. If you do, I'll have to ask you to leave."

"Oh, sure," one of the Marines replied, and they walked into the reception room.

Evidently, as the hours passed and the whiskey flowed, several of the Marines became belligerent and began causing trouble. The bouncer calmly walked over to one of loudest of them and said, "Son, you have got to hold it down, or I'm going to ask you to leave." The warning was ignored, and after a few minutes, the bouncer was back.

"Young man, come with me. You need to leave the building."

"What? Naw, I ain't ready to go."

"I said, come with me!"

"Make me."

Evidently, the Marine, who had been fighting Germans for several years, didn't think a bouncer in an Arkansas bordello was much of a threat. However, he was mistaken. The last thing the Marine said was, "Ahaaaa!" as he was thrown down the stairs. His buddies rushed after him and carried away a serviceman with his pride severely wounded.

And, as a side note about those stairs: Lee Ann said when she remodeled the building, she had to replace all of the treads because of wear from the countless shoes and boots who had made good use of them.

Spirits

The general consensus, from Lee Ann Herndon, is that not one but several spirits occupy the old bordello. At different times (and recognized by several people) they are: Betty Fortenberry (the madam), the bouncer (name unknown), Blondie the prostitute, and a young girl from 5 to 7 years old (not named). Each of these have in various ways made themselves known, not to just Lee Ann but also to others who have either worked in the store or lived in the apartments.

One of the most shocking and dramatic sightings was made by Lee Ann's brother. He stopped by the business one afternoon and after visiting with Lee Ann, walked to the office at the back of the store.

"Who's the young girl sitting on the desk?" he called out as he leaned back out of the door to talk with Lee Ann.

"There's no young girl in here," replied Lee Ann.

Her brother turned and looked; she was gone. He almost left the place.

Jeff Ulmer, who currently lives in one of the upstairs apartments, is also certain that spirits are present. He has heard and felt the presence of several, including disembodied female voices. These occur daily, along with noises of thumping and rumbling in the next room, which he uses as storage.

Of course, no one is ever there. Occasionally an item will suddenly fly off the wall and seemly be yanked to the floor. And there is a feeling, this tenant says, that you are not alone, even when no one else is in the apartment.

Jeff is also convinced that the haunting is not confined to the old former Crystal Hotel. He recounts a spirit making itself known several hundred yards west of the hotel as it pecked on a window at a nearby South Arkansas University classroom. After my investigation of the downtown buildings, I certainly concur with Jeff—the entire downtown area is home to hundreds of spirits.

Lee Ann recounts numerous times when tools disappeared after she had just laid them down, only to show up minutes later exactly where she had put them. She mentioned several men who worked on the upstairs apartments, and quit after a series of unexplained sounds permeated the workplace. And, of course, there have been countless footsteps on empty stairs, the scent of perfume, unexplained shadows on the walls, and several other appearances (glimpses) of the young girl. She also mentions how objects suddenly fly across the room, very much like those described by Jeff Ulmer, who lives upstairs.

A psychic visited the building several years back and immediately recognized the madam. She had this comment to Lee Ann—from the madam. "I like what you are doing to the building, but not your boyfriend."

Lee Ann thought that was strange, but a few months later, after a painful breakup, she realized the madam was right about the boyfriend.

In my opinion, of all the places I have investigated while writing this book, The Crystal Hotel comes in at almost the top of the list. Only the Rialto Theater surpasses this old bordello in the presence of paranormal occurrences.

21

THE OLYMPIC BILLIARD PARLOR AND THE RUNNERS

ACROSS the street and a half block down from the Rialto Theater there is a large two-story building with a colorful past. Today the building is home to two places: La Piazza, an Italian restaurant, and, on the second floor, Einstein's, a jazz and dance club. But early in its history, that building was one of the most notorious spots in El Dorado.

When I was a boy, just the mention of the Olympic Billiard Parlor was enough to have me asking my dad about the fights and the famous baseball bat-swinging bartender. Well, to 12- and 13-year-old boys, he was famous. We called him "Slugger" because of the baseball bat he used to break-up fights. He was a thin, little man, completely bald, who didn't weigh 130 pounds. He walked around with a cigarette hanging out of his mouth.

He might have been a skinny, little man, but he had an equalizer in the form of a sawed-off, Louisville Slugger baseball bat that he used to break up fights. The Olympic had a big, open main floor and a long bar that extended nearly all the way across the west wall of the building. The bar was made of a very dark—almost black—wood, complete with a brass foot rail and spittoons on either end.

Every time I looked in, the bar would be full of men and the smoke would be so thick I could barely see across the room. Most of the main room had pool tables with old, green light fixtures hanging over each table.

Of course, with all the beer and whiskey that was served at the bar, fights were common. I remember standing out in front of the double saloon doors, peeking in through the crack and hearing cursing, then threats, and—sooner or later—a fight that usually sent one of the men spinning back into the pool tables.

As soon as the fight started, Slugger would reach under the bar and come out with his bat. The bat was about half size and about 3 inches in diameter. It was big enough for Slugger to wheel around with one hand, and he'd hit anything and everything that had a part in the fight—hands, arms, legs, and heads. Of course, even the biggest and toughest of the guys fighting backed off when Slugger waded in swinging. Many stories were told of drunken roughnecks from the oilfields, who drank and fought until a lick from Slugger's bat put them away. Many were maimed for life and several never regained consciousness.

Most of the action occurred on the main downstairs floor, but the Olympic had a lot more going on than just drinking, playing pool, and fighting. About a third of the downstairs—the back third—was raised about 3 feet with a rail around it. That area was also open, and it was filled with domino tables. Moon was the game of choice and there was always money on the table. There wasn't really a full second floor; it was a mezzanine about 6 feet wide that extended completely around the interior of the building. There were rooms off the west side, but the doors were always shut and locked.

The mezzanine was my place to hang out while my dad had a beer at the bar. I have often wondered what went on behind the closed doors on the west side of the mezzanine. The smell of perfume wafted through the air and laughter and giggles seemed to flow out of those rooms.

I think those rooms have tales to tell, and, naturally, since almost every building that had upstairs rooms served as a bordello,

I am relatively sure these Olympic rooms were just another place where prostitutes plied their trade. Of course, as a somewhat naïve 12-year-old, I didn't have a clue about what went on there. I was only interested in the action on the main floor, and rarely was I disappointed.

After the Olympic Billiard Parlor went out of business in the late 1950s, the building became part of the old Sample's Department Store, and during that time the upstairs mezzanine and the rooms on the west side were used for storage. One of the former high school workers told me this story.

"All of the boxes and bags for the store were in the two rooms on the west side of the old Olympic mezzanine. That was the creepiest place I've ever been in. There where racks out in the middle of the room and shelves on the wall. Several things bothered me and after working there a while, I started bringing someone along when I went to get boxes or bags. It was always something; sometimes the boxes would fall off the shelves, or other times they would be in a different place than I had put them, but the spookiest thing was the breeze that would hit me when I opened the door to these rooms. There were no vents or windows, but air would be moving.

"Sometimes I could smell stale beer and cigarettes. Other times, perfume. They had painted these rooms with a thin coat of white paint, but you could still see what was written on the old walls. I don't remember much, but I do remember some women's names and in one area there were numbers and what looked like figures—you know—money." (Pretty good evidence of another brothel, I think.)

On the main floor of the adjacent building to the west, Sample's Department Store had an appliance center called Sample's Electrical City. The first TV I ever saw was in the window of that store. According to one of my sources, Sample's finally had to stop using this part of the building because of undetermined electrical problems. I've often wondered if the spirits of the Olympic Billiard Parlor are still in the building, and if they had anything to do with those electrical problems.

After Sample's closed the Electrical City part of their store, the Olympic building was home to the local telephone company who extended the mezzanine and made a complete second floor. Evidently, the phone company also had problems because of reasons that never were very clear; the company dropped its lease after spending thousands of dollars in remodeling costs.

After the phone company left, I purchased the building, and ripped out the dozens of small offices to create an open space where Rookies, a sports bar, located. Later, the business was purchased by Kelvin Warwick, and after extensive structural work an upstairs dance club called Einstein's opened.. Over the past few years, as the building was renovated, several workers have noted strange sounds coming from the upstairs; and even in the back stairwell that formerly went to the mezzanine, unusual things have happened.

How many of the early 1920s oil-boom murders occurred in or just outside of the Olympic, or what really did go on in the upstairs rooms just off the mezzanine? How many men did Slugger injure or actually kill with his baseball bat? One thing for sure, if any place in town has a reason to be haunted, it's the old Olympic Billiard Parlor.

Do spirits still reside in the old building that is now La Piazza, an Italian restaurant? If you ask some of the patrons or the current operators of the upstairs dance club, they would tell you "yes," and then they would relay stories about lights flickering, doors slamming, and the sudden smell of perfume. And last but not least, they would recount the night where a puff of white mist drifted into the room—Vapor from the ice machine? No one thinks so. But one Saturday night, after the doors were closed and only two employees were still in the main room, this white mist did float down the stairs that went to the back of the building. The two workers were startled and began to back away, but just as quick as it had appeared, the mist disappeared.

The story of the Olympic would not be complete without mentioning the Runners who were always out front waiting for a drunken, oilfield worker to leave the bar. The Runners, as they were called, were put in place in the late 1920s, after the oil-boom peaked. For the first couple of years after the boom started, South Washington Avenue, Cedar Street, and Locust Street contained an estimated 25 brothels. Most of these houses of ill repute were in the gambling houses or barrelhouses that lined South Washington Avenue, also known as Hamburger Row. Almost every building in this section of town with upstairs rooms housed prostitutes. The row of barrelhouses extended south to Hillsboro Street, but that area was by no means the only place in the county where barrelhouses could be found.

In the 1920s, and even today, Hillsboro Street, a couple of blocks south of the Rialto Theater, was and is, the primary east-west street in the city. During the 1920s Hillsboro Street was dirt with a mix of gravel. It became nearly impassable after a good rain. The muleskinners drove their steel-rimmed wagons, pulled by as many as 20 mules or oxen, down the street heading west toward the first oilfield in Arkansas, the El Dorado Field. The street drops off about a half-mile west of town and crosses a low area that back in the 1920s was a small creek.

In the 1920s, the hill was so difficult to navigate up that after a rain, a team of mules was stationed at the bottom of the hill, and for $3 you could have your car pulled up the slick, red mud hill. Your other choice was to park it in an area that became known as Death Valley and return the next day and pick up a stripped automobile.

The hill received the name "Pistol Hill" for obvious reasons, and the small creek and valley below became "Death Valley" because of the number of knifings that occurred around the barrelhouses in the area. Death Valley was only a few hundred yards away from the famous Busey Well, and it attracted hundreds of visitors each day to view the working site. Well, where there were large crowds, they were women and gambling. And even though this was in the middle of prohibition, moonshine whiskey flowed freely from dozens of saloons.

However, the crackdown by law enforcement officials that came during the mid- to late-1920s, made it a little harder for prostitutes to solicit on the street, and the gambling was suppressed. But the wide-open gambling and prostitution certainly didn't stop; it just went behind closed doors. Very few of the brothels actually closed, but because they were not able to openly solicit customers on the street or stand in front of their establishment beckoning their potential customers, the prostitutes' business dropped off appreciably.

Clever madams, however, came up with a way to solicit by using a very unlikely method. Young African-American boys from around the age of 16 were recruited to be runners for the various houses of prostitution. These young men were paid one dollar for each customer that followed them to the various houses.

The young men were not pimps. They had no connection with the prostitutes, for whom they were soliciting. They were on commission and worked directly for the madam of each brothel.

The going commission was one dollar per man, but that solicited man had to enter the brothel in order for the boys to get paid. And since they only got paid for men who followed them into the brothels, the runners were always coming up with stories of how beautiful the girls were. And to prove it, they produced pictures of gorgeous women—who naturally weren't the prostitutes in the bordellos the young men were soliciting for. Nevertheless, they used these pictures—and anything else they could conjure up—to entice the men.

Naturally, the price of the services the ladies were offering was discussed, and the young runners always had a story.

"Today, instead of five dollars the price is only two!"

Or: *"They will let you have two girls for the price of one, but that's just for today."*

Well, of course, when the men saw the gorgeous pictures of women, and then heard how the price had been suddenly reduced, they were anxious to enter the brothel. However, when a potential customer followed a runner into one of the brothels, the madam met the man, and, of course, she ignored the stories about $2 sex, as well as the inevitable question: *"Where is the beautiful girl in the picture?"* But as free whiskey flowed and scantily clad girls paraded through, the men usually forgot all about it. And if those enticements weren't enough, one or more of the lovelies would caress the customer and sit in his lap.

Three elderly, African-American men living in El Dorado today were Runners during the late 1920s, and they remember very well the details of their job and where they solicited. They worked the town south of Main Street, even venturing out Hillsboro Street to Death Valley and Pistol Hill. The hijackers were still very active in the areas where the Runners worked, but these young men never were accosted. The hijackers didn't want to bother with young boys who never had more than a few dollars on them.

If any Runners ventured north of Main or around the courthouse, the police would chase them back south to Cedar Street or South Washington Avenue. Their job was to solicit men—especially oilfield workers who had just been paid, and were looking for a little entertainment.

It was a simple, effective way to get business for the many brothels that were operating in town. Since the county sheriff's office and city police department were woefully undermanned, law and order was confined to a block around the courthouse square. Of course, with the mayhem on Hamburger Row from criminals, illegal gambling, drinking, and prostitution, the average El Dorado citizen did everything he or she could do to keep from going into the area after dark. And even in the best residential sections of town it was common practice to bar and lock your door at 5 p.m. and not open it again until daylight.

Yes, in the 1920s it was common knowledge around town that numerous bordellos operated on South Washington Avenue and Cedar Street, but the law looked the other way. It would be that way for nearly 40 years.

22

THE OLD PRESBYTERIAN CEMETERY AND THE SLAVE – GHOSTS OF SOUTH WASHINGTON AVENUE

SOME of the paranormal occurrences and strange happenings in and around the Rialto Theater would be difficult to explain if we didn't delve into the history of El Dorado's first cemetery, the old Presbyterian Cemetery on South Washington Avenue. Confederate soldiers lie next to women who were lost in childbirth and babies who died of Yellow Fever. And if there's ever to be a who's who of Union County leaders from the mid-1800s, you can be certain it will consist of the town's early residents who are buried there.

As in most early Southern cemeteries, many of the family plots have elaborate wrought iron fences and beautiful gates to designate a family's sacred ground. Some years, at Halloween, the Union County Historical Society stages a historical reenactment in the cemetery, with the Society members dressed in period costumes. It all seems so historical and serene, even though many of the re-enactors have commented on strange sounds, unaccounted-for mists, and other paranormal activities, especially along the east side of the boundary fence, which is the back of the cemetery. However, most residents of South Arkansas just consider this old graveyard to be nothing more than a relic of the past.

Ah, but there is more—much more. And this time the macabre facts were documented by an eyewitness. One of the most horrific incidents the town ever experienced occurred a few years after the start of the oil boom of the 1920s. It was so repulsive that evidently the citizens who witnessed it formed a bond to never discuss it, or tell any of the detail of this horrific event. However, we have an eyewitness account from the son of a man who was on the site when this desecration occurred.

It was the removal and destruction of not one but dozens of graves from a known cemetery. And I believe it happened because of the greed spawned by the oil boom and the need to accommodate additional businesses that were coming to El Dorado.

To understand why this happened, we must look back at the train arrivals and departures to and from El Dorado before and after the oil boom. Before the discovery of oil, there were two train arrivals and departures per day, with each train consisting of two coaches. The small Missouri Pacific railroad station was located on the south edge of town, just east of the Presbyterian Cemetery. After all, with a population of only 3,800, two train arrivals and departures a day were sufficient for the city.

However, with the discovery of oil on Jan. 10, 1921, came a crush of humanity, and it overwhelmed the town. The population swelled to more than 50,000 during only the second year of the boom.

Within that time period, the number of train arrivals and departures increased to 22 a day, and instead of two passenger coaches, these trains had between 10 and 12 passenger coaches, all packed with newcomers to El Dorado. Obviously, the small station was much too small to handle this influx, and leading citizens of El Dorado met to plan an expansion of the main station. According to some sources, they initially recommended building a new station south of town where ample land was available, but evidently the barrelhouse owners along South Washington Avenue—across from the existing station—cajoled and, some say, bribed the committee. So, with the help of the railroads involved, city leaders decided to build a new station where the small old station stood.

However, there was just one problem with the location. In order to build the size of building needed and to have ample loading and unloading facilities, planners needed much more land than was available along the railroad right-of-way. The plans for the new station were probably hatched in a back-room meeting—something El Dorado is famous for even today—but, regardless, a plan was developed to acquire enough land to accommodate the new station. And that land, only a block south of the Rialto, became the scene of the most detestable occurrences in the City of El Dorado's history.

According to local accounts, part of the land needed was of questionable title, because when the property for the Presbyterian Cemetery was deeded for use as a cemetery, part of the land that became part of the extended cemetery was never deeded to the church or the city. The cemetery is a block south of the Rialto Theater on South Washington Avenue, and it's also one of the oldest cemeteries in Union County. It has numerous graves dating back before the Civil War.

According to local lore, the cemetery was first opened when the county was settled in early 1840s, during the days of slavery, and after a few years, members of the white community began to bury some of their trusted and loyal slaves in an open plot of ground immediately east and adjacent to the white cemetery. Soon it became known as the Colored Cemetery, and dozens of new graves were added each year. By the early 1920s, both the white and colored cemeteries were almost full and a new cemetery was opened east of town on a large tract of land.

During the time that the so-called Colored Cemetery was in use, a wire fence was built around it, a few marble headstones were erected, and metal crosses dotted many graves. Of course, there were also many unmarked graves of poor souls whose owners or families wouldn't or couldn't buy headstones. So they were interred without coffins or stones, and many times they were laid to rest in multiple graves.

When the Colored Cemetery reached capacity and closed, it became weed- infested and trashed. It was now the subject of discussion by the committee charged with building the new railroad station.

A plan showing the new station and loading facilities was immediately accepted, but then the problem of too little land surfaced. The proposed overlay of the station and the necessary docks and parking areas covered all of the Colored Cemetery. Of course, everyone on the committee noticed it immediately, and a discussion about what to do started. The following dialogue is an approximation of the rumored discussion, as reported by several individuals.

"Hell, boys, they's a bunch of coloreds buried right where y'all have the station spotted. What in the hell are you gonna do about that?"

Well, of course that was a sticky question and no one present was willing to do the obvious and suggest that the cemetery be moved at the city's expense. So the discussion continued until someone said, "Y'all know how much that would cost? Why it would be thousands of dollars just to move the graves we know about, and what about all them unmarked graves? Hell, we'd be spending money like water. We gotta come up with somethin' else."

Naturally, a meeting such as this one could not be kept secret, and soon it was common knowledge that the city fathers were discussing where to put the new railroad station. The problem of the old Colored Cemetery was noted as the holdup that would stop the station from being built close into town and, naturally, near the row of barrelhouses on Hamburger Row.

The account below is only a guess at how the graveyard desecration occurred. This account is based on the lawless times associated with the early years of the oil boom.

Of course, as the many trains emptied the hordes of get-rich-quick speculators, the barrelhouses were furnished with ready customers. When some of the owners of those establishments heard that the alternate site for the station was more than a half-mile south they decided to send an emissary to attempt to keep the new station downtown. They picked the most ruthless and influential of their group.

Enter Jake, the owner of Jake's Place the biggest and wildest barrelhouse on Hamburger Row. According to rumors, he'd heard about the meeting to find land to build the new station, and since Jake's Place was immediately across the street from the proposed station, site Jake entered the meeting with a plan to have the new station built exactly where the old one was located—only bigger and with more docks for freight and passengers. As the passengers exited the coach cars, they would be looking across the street at Jake's Place. Business was always good when the train unloaded thirsty passengers from Little Rock or Shreveport.

"Gentlemen, I believe I have a solution to the problem," Jake said as the distinguished city leader squirmed uneasily in their seats. Jake was well known in El Dorado and his reputation was horrible. He was rumored to be financing a gang of hijackers that preyed on the unsuspecting oilfield workers when they came into El Dorado after working weeks out in the oilfields, ready to spend their money for a good time. Many times the walk back to the workers' tents, which were pitched west of town, ended up with the naive men being picked up in the mortuary wagon, which made the rounds of the alleys off Hamburger Row every Saturday and Sunday morning.

But instead of asking Jake to leave, these men took a deep breath and waited for him to lay out his plan. They knew from past experience that if Jake wanted something, he had the muscle to have it done. His solution might not be the most up and up way to solve the problem, but it was sure to be a solution. And they knew Jake wasn't going to beat around the bush. His plan would be laid out with all the details in seconds, but when Jake spoke the directness and the depth of the plan surprised even the men who knew him best.

"*Give me about six hours next Sunday morning, and I'll have you a cleaned-off site big enough for a new station, and it'll be right where we want it—where the old station is now.*"

"*Now, Jake, you know they ain't room there, 'cause we done looked and tried everything to site that damn station there. It can't be done.*"

"*Sure it can, and here's a sketch of the site with the new station on it.*" Jake unrolled a map and, sure enough, there was a big new station drawn out with a large passenger area and big offloading docks for all the oilfield equipment that came in by train. There was a look of surprise and then a collective gasp as the men realized what Jake was proposing.

"*My God, Jake, you're putting most of the station right on top of that old Colored Cemetery!*"

"*So?*"

"*Well, hell Jake, folks just won't stand for that.*"

"*Who won't stand for it? Well, ain't y'all the men that run this crappie little town? Don't you think I can get rid of that eyesore by noon Sunday?*"

There was a stunned silence as the men glanced nervously around at each other and then H. C. Donnybaker, a banker said, "*Uh, Jake, we done looked into moving all them graves and, hell, it'd cost a fortune. Just how're you gonna move them?*"

Of course, H. C. knew Jake had no intention of doing grave relocation, but he just couldn't make himself face the obvious.

"Boys, I'm going to replant them in the Ouachita River, and I'll be through before y'all get outta church."

Every man knew exactly what Jake was proposing, but they had been too ashamed to ask.

"Hell, boys, y'all know that damn Colored Cemetery is just an eyesore and the land it's on don't belong to nobody. And you know as well as I do that there won't be a soul who'll complain. If they do, then I'll have my boys talk with them, and I can assure you they won't complain again."

Jake bit down on his thin, black cigar and grinned at the stone-faced men sitting around the table.

There was a minute of silence until Jake said, *"Well, if there's no objections I'll have 25 men, a couple of them big, dirt-moving machines they uses to build oil well locations, and a bunch of hauling wagons all ready to start moving dirt at daylight Sunday. Now, boys, if y'all have any problems with that you had better say so now, 'cause it'll be too late Sunday morning. Sheriff, do you understand that?"*

There was a nod of silent agreement.

"Fine! Now when church is over just come by and look at the new, cleaned-off site for the new station." Jake rolled up his drawing, turned, and left the meeting.

After another few minutes, the meeting broke up without a single man raising any objection to what would be the most macabre chapter of El Dorado history. By Sunday, Jake had rounded up his crews and the horrible job of desecrating a cemetery began.

Note: *This above recounting of the desecration of the old slave cemetery is taken from the following account. The person giving the account was lucid and detailed in his description of what happened.*

However, the location of the cemetery was not mentioned in the story his father told him. The above recounting is only my guess as to the location Mr. Alderson refers to, and, of course, the men mentioned and the dialogue are strictly fictional. However, as you will note below an event such as mentioned above did happen.

Boyd Alderson, who was 92 when he told this story to his son, Edwin, remembers his father coming in and telling about the incident. According to this eyewitness—Boyd's father—early that morning a large crew met with an unnamed contractor who brought heavy equipment to the cemetery. The equipment operators knew their job and soon the big, earth-moving equipment had plowed up dozens of graves. Boyd's father mentioned seeing partly decomposed bodies, pieces of wooden coffins, and headstones all being removed and hauled off.

Some of the crew, who had no idea they would be doing such a horrific task, refused to finish the job, and the final movement of the graves was handled by assorted riffraff from South Washington Avenue who were paid $20 each for a morning's work.

Several workers confided to their friends that the destruction of the cemetery was an eerie undertaking. It was just before dawn when the work started and soon the air became heavy with the stench of decomposing bodies, which made the work almost unbearable. As the heavy, excavating machines worked, their metal blades scraped against the tombstones, making a scream-like sound. There was no attempt to re-bury the bodies of men, women, and even small children that day, and load after load of dirt—filled with skeletons, partially decomposed bodies, parts of wooden coffins, and grave markers—left the area in the backs of trucks to be dumped in the Ouachita River near the small town of Calion.

Of course, my elaboration of the story, as repeated by Boyd Alderson, is an extrapolation of the event, and should not be taken as part of his statement. In order to give the readers of this book a better understanding of this piece of oil-boom history, I have added fiction to the placement and activities that resulted in the removal of these graves. The above account is not to be taken as a historical recounting of an event—except for the testimony of Boyd Alderson.

That would seem to be all of the story, but according to some people strange events began to occur in the railroad area around the old cemetery and even up to, and in, the Rialto Theater that was just a block away. Soon people began to suspect the cemetery's desecration had brought forth spirits from the disturbed graves. Late at night, strange sounds were heard from the station area and even from the back of the Rialto Theater. Did the ghosts from the desecrated Colored Cemetery move into the theater when the graveyard was destroyed? Some think so, and several of the apparitions have been of men and women of color.

There were also reports of someone, or something, rattling the outside back door of the theater—the door with "concessions" written on it. And, of course, even when someone was standing there looking, nothing was ever seen. However, more than one person has noticed fresh dirt by the door, and several have said it seems more than one "something" is present—maybe three or four at one time. Some say it is the spirits from the old Colored Cemetery who lost their home and are looking to inhabit a new dwelling.

Well, whatever the reason for these supernatural occurrences, not many brave souls have been able to spend any time behind the theater in the dark of the moon without being "spooked."

After the removal of the old cemetery was finished, the work on the new train station began, and the El Dorado business community tried to forget the horrible crime they had sanctioned. Almost immediately, however, stories began to unfold of strange, paranormal activities occurring during the building of the new railroad station. Timber fell from the partially constructed ceiling, injuring several men. Mysterious sounds seemed to be everywhere, and sightings of strange apparitions were commonplace.

The work continued 24 hours a day, seven days a week, until the station was finished. However, no sooner than it had been dedicated, night clerks and stationmasters began to tell appalling stories of strange paranormal apparitions, sometimes even including body parts. This continued up until the 1970s when the station was leveled because of the reduced number of trains, but was it really leveled because of the frequent haunting and the trouble the railroad had keeping workers on the job after dark? That question remains in the dustbin of El Dorado history.

After the station was torn down, ghost sightings around the old cemetery seemed to cease, but just when everyone thought they had seen the last of paranormal activities in the area, reports began to come in about strange happenings around the back of the Rialto Theater, just a block away. Did the ghosts from the old desecrated cemetery move a block north and take up residence in the basement of the theater, as some have suggested, or did the spirits from the old Colored Cemetery move into the remaining white section that remained.

The only logical explanation is that there are probably more than one reason for this concentration of paranormal occurrences. These reasons would include: slave ghosts from the old slave cemetery; oilfield workers who were killed by hijackers; innocent men who went to the gallows; and slain prostitutes who died behind the theater. Have these spirits gathered in this area?

Carol Pate, the psychic who investigated the theater, seems to agree that something caused a concentration of spirits in the old basement and vaudeville dressing rooms at the very back of the theater. Pate was overwhelmed by the vast numbers of spirits in this area; in fact, and they were so intense that the numbers overcame her.

Has the Rialto become a place of spirit clusters? Maybe. It seems this ancient cemetery was in the way of progress and jobs for the city, and even though what happened was against the law of the State of Arkansas, no one was ever charged or prosecuted for the crime. The local newspaper never mentioned it. With all the chaos going on with the oil boom, the desecration of a cemetery was quickly forgotten, and it has remained one of El Dorado's darkest secrets ever since.

23

MULESKINNER'S CORNER ON HAMBURGER ROW

In the early days of the oil boom, many more sinister activities took place along the portion of South Washington Avenue known as Hamburger Row than bad hamburgers. The street was lined with saloons or barrelhouses, as they were called in the early 1920s. In the early years of the oil boom, 1921 and 1922, every one of the buildings along Hamburger Row featured wide-open gambling, prostitution, and sales of liquor, and drugs—all illegal. The only two pieces of real estate that didn't have a cheap, wooden barrelhouse on it were the old Presbyterian Cemetery, where many of the leading citizens of early El Dorado found their final resting place, and the corner of South Washington Avenue and Hillsboro Street, which was called Muleskinners Corner.

During the 1920s, a plot of land roughly the size of a city block was a temporary home to hundreds of mules and oxen that were that were harnessed each day to haul heavy equipment to the oilfields. Each morning, some of the toughest and most ruthless men in the city practiced their trade here. My wife's grandfather was one of those muleskinners (mule drivers) during the oil boom, and he drove a team of 20 oxen as he hauled equipment to the Smackover Oil Field.

The muleskinners were some of the most rugged men who worked in the South Arkansas oilfields. The primary driver sat on the wagon seat and, depending on the number of mules or oxen, as many as three additional muleskinners stood spaced out on the traces to whip and guide the team. Saying that they were a rough bunch is an understatement.

Naturally, when a group of men who are of that mindset and disposition competed for work every morning, fights broke out, and more than one fight left bodies in the mud. And, since that intersection is the lowest part of South Washington Avenue, and a good South Arkansas downpour would send torrents of water down the street—which didn't have underground drainage—the ground where they hitched up their teams was usually a quagmire.

After the fighting and bargaining for a load, the muleskinners would usually head north toward the Smackover Field, approximately 10 miles away, or west to the El Dorado Field. There were two routes available, if you were heading for Smackover; you went a block west and then made a right onto South West Avenue, or just went straight north up South Washington Avenue.

Since the only paved streets ended a block from the Courthouse Square, almost all of the hauling was over dirt and gravel roads. Even during dry weather, the big, iron wagon wheels rutted the streets so badly that the streets were difficult to cross, and if it rained, they became almost impassable. Stories of mules drowning in the streets in some of the giant mud holes have been told many times, and there are numerous pictures to prove it.

Dragging the heavy equipment up Hamburger Row rutted the street so badly that entrepreneurs built wooden sidewalks to lower across the street for pedestrians to cross —for 25 cents. But, during a time when everything seemed for sale, it was just accepted as the way things were.

In order to understand how the muleskinners and oilmen plied their trade, I have included an excerpt from my novel, *The Queen of Hamburger Row:*

Hays provided the excitement with a spectacular rig move. Saturday morning, when the town was full of people, he hired two teams of 20 oxen each down at Muleskinner's Corner. Then he loaded the entire set of drilling equipment onto two, big tandem wagons, and at noon, he headed for Main Street, to loop through downtown before heading west to the drill site.

Almost every rig move to the oilfields went in the opposite direction from downtown, heading west on Hillsboro Street, usually with five small loads of equipment. Of course, as soon as Hays's wagons pulled out into the Hamburger Row traffic, which consisted of wagons, small trucks, and an assortment of cars, he caused a huge traffic jam. The muleskinners standing in the traces were cursing up a blue streak and anything with a horn on it was blaring. Black whips were cracking across the mules' backs and the ruckus could be heard through most of downtown.

Hays had told Sylvia and Masha about the rig move the night before, and they were standing on the front steps of Jake's Place, watching for him, when they saw the oxen turn down Hamburger Row and head north to Main Street. To Masha, the boilers, mud pumps, draw-works, and other pieces of drilling equipment that were inching their way up the street looked like a mountain of steel. Two big tandem flatbed wagons, each with six wheels, were being pulled by two teams of 20 oxen driven by three muleskinners, who were spaced out, standing on the traces, cracking long black whips and spewing cuss words as they guided the teams. The big wagons took up most of the street, and, although moving oilfield equipment up Hamburger Row was nothing out of the ordinary, the size of the wagons and the two teams of oxen were more than most people had ever seen. It was quite a sight.

"My God, look at that!" said Masha. "Hays is sitting on the wagon with the muleskinner!"

She felt a little shiver run through her when she thought about Bill actually owning a part of the drilling operation that would be starting up very soon. The mountain of equipment that was passing by gave her hope.

Hays was sitting up on the wagon with the team driver, and occasionally he would stand up to wave.

"Hey, Masha, Sylvia, how's this for movin' in a rig?" The big wagons made Hamburger Row a one-way street. Traffic stopped, people gawked, and Hays yelled to the crowd of oil promoters who had walked out of the Garrett Hotel lobby to watch.

"Headin' for the #1 Stocks! Gonna spud tomorrow!" But as the wagons neared the paved part of the street a block off Main Street, he was stopped by a police officer.

"Damn it!" the officer screamed at Hays, "you can't bring those wagons down Main Street with those iron-rimmed wheels; you'll tear up this new street!" The city of El Dorado had paved the area around the square with concrete and had recently extended the paving to one block off the square. The local police didn't give a damn about the crime on Hamburger Row, but tearing up a newly paved street was a different matter.

There was so much noise from the muleskinners, the crowds, and the honking horns that Hays was able to act as if he couldn't hear the police officer. The muleskinners cracked their whips and the teams lurched forward, moving onto Main Street with the iron-rimmed wheels cutting into the new concrete. Soon they were out of sight, and 45-minutes later, Hays showed up back at the Garrett Hotel, talking up the new well. The rig move through town had caused had quite a stir, and Hays managed to sell another 5,000 shares in his open-ended trust.

***

As I did my research on the area and heard stories about the mayhem of the oil boom—the dozens of houses of ill-repute, open drinking, and gambling during Prohibition—I became aware that the political leadership and the men and women in other official positions in the city, knew, sanctioned, and lied about the crime that infested the town. In interview after interview, I was met with copious denials about anything that would besmirch the character of the city. The murders on Hamburger Row, prostitution, gambling, and drinking were all systematically denied.

"No, El Dorado has always been a quiet town, even in the oil boom," one elderly gentleman told me. Well, if El Dorado was such a quiet town, then why did the local mortuaries send wagons down to Hamburger Row, Pistol Hill, and Death Valley on weekends to pick up bodies? And why were there so few police records of the hundreds of documented murders that eyewitnesses reported? There is only one answer: The leading citizens of the community, the ones with enough influence to suppress reports about the thousands of acts of illegal activities, wanted to preserve the impression that El Dorado was a peaceful, quiet community—and they also wanted to keep the illegal activities available for their entertainment.

Or maybe there's more to the story than just the idea that El Dorado leaders were determined to preserve the image of the town. Were these men involved in the illegal activities? Were the various police and other law enforcement officials being paid off? I guess we'll never know, but according to various witnesses, a number of these same leading citizens were spotted frequenting the Randolph Hotel.

Were they there to have dinner or to have a drink at the Petroleum Club? Or, as some asserted (after peering from upstairs windows in the Garrett Hotel across the street) were these men really there to be serviced by the prostitutes.

24

THE SPIRITS OF OIL HERITAGE PARK

IT would be hard to find a plot of ground in downtown El Dorado that has had more history connected to it than the quarter block on the corner of Jefferson Avenue and Cedar Street. The list of shady businesses located on this quarter block, the hundreds of murders where the victims were found sprawled in the adjoining alley, and stories about executions on the old oak tree (and later the gallows) could fill a large book. Today this serene piece of real estate belies its past, and statues in Oil Heritage Park overlook an ordinary parking lot

However, a look back at the history of this small plot of ground reveals some tragic and horrific activities that would shock even the most hardened person. This 100-by-100-foot lot was the stage for a panorama of bloody, abhorrent El Dorado history played out violently during the past 150 years.

It all started in the mid 1840s when vigilante justice was carried out by hanging convicted men from the limb of a massive oak tree. This oak tree, rumored to be the largest tree in the area, was on the corner of the lot, immediately behind what is now the Black Cat Cafe. Later, this makeshift gallows was replaced by a rickety, wooden structure made of logs and rough-cut planks. Executions too numerous to count were carried out from the gallows that were in use from the mid 1840s until 1912. (Arkansas law mandated that anyone who was given the death penalty be hanged in the county where the crime was committed, if a proper gallows was available.)

One local resident told me that her great-grandmother was an eyewitness to executions carried out on the Union County gallows. Others residents confirmed stories about the gallows, and their comments indicated that the gallows were used frequently during the county's early days. In fact, during the early settlement of Union County, there was an official, part-time hangman. Strange stories—all relating to executed criminals—abound, since frontier justice was anything but fair. Naturally, some of the convicted felons, who were about to be executed, threatened the law enforcement officials with retribution, promising to return from the grave to seek justice.

But, there is more blood and tragedy associated with this lot than just the misfortune of convicted criminals who were hanged from the old oak tree and the gallows. After the state began to assume the job of executing convicted men, the gallows were removed, and the lot was left vacant. It was still a vacant lot in the early 1900s when the bloody Tucker-Parnell gunfight took place a block away on Jefferson Avenue. Three men were killed and three men were wounded in the bloody gunfight, which kicked off a horrific feud and took the lives of some 20 men.

In 1902, Jefferson Avenue was a mixture of gravel and dirt. After the gunfight in front of the old, redbrick Victorian courthouse, and across the street in front of the Arcade Hotel, there were bloody puddles of blood in the dirt and gravel.

Of course, as the rumors go, city leaders wanted to get rid of any evidence of the violent conflict, so they immediately dug up the bloody dirt and gravel, and replaced the bloodstained dirt with fresh dirt and gravel. And what did the men do with the bloody soil? Of course, they dumped it in the nearest vacant lot where the old gallows once stood—on the corner of Jefferson Avenue and Cedar Street.

Evidently, from my review of old city directories, there were no substantial businesses on the lot until the oil boom of the early 1920s was in full swing. Immediately after the first wells came in, a row of shoddy barrelhouses quickly popped up along Cedar Street, each with a bar and gambling tables on the first floor and a bordello on the second. Naturally, the clientele that flooded these establishments contributed to the violence associated with the barrelhouses, but the knifings and shootings attributed to the rowdy bunch in the barrelhouses were only the tip of a ghastlier arrangement.

As crowds of men left the barrelhouses and surged up from Hamburger Row and Cedar Street toward the courthouse area—where tents and other lodgings were available—they had to walk past the alleyway that separated the south and north half of the block. During the first few years of the oil boom, these 200 feet, from the southeast corner of the block north toward Main Street, were easiest the most dangerous 200 feet in the city. And the alleyways behind the buildings along Main Street were tagged with the name "Death Alley."

Always lurking in these dark, mid-block alleyways were the notorious hijackers, as the oilfield hands called them, and, woe be it if a green hand, not realizing the danger, decided to walk up to the Courthouse Square by himself. He would not only be robbed but killed.

I interviewed one elderly gentlemen who was well into his 90s. He told me the hijackers killed most of their victims with knives. Even though the hijackers were mainly out to rob, they killed most of their victims. It was usually three or four men with knives, who stabbed and then cut the throats of the men and the occasional prostitute, stripped them of anything of value, and then dragged them into the alleyways. The next morning, the mortuary wagon would stop by the alley and haul victims back to the funeral home.

Some of the alleyways, especially the one behind the stores on Main Street, carried the nickname "Death Alley" and for good reason. The following is an excerpt from my novel, *The Queen of Hamburger Row*. It vividly illustrates the dangers lurking in the alleyway around Hamburger Row.

..."Drinks are on me, boys! I'm on a roll tonight!" he hollered to the men sitting at the bar. He handed Shug a $20 bill and said, "Keep 'um comin' till this runs out."

After Sylvia gave Slim the drink, she walked back to the bar and watched as he cleaned out the players at the crap table. When Slim finished playing, she glanced over at the door to the back room, where a stocky, rough-looking man was standing. She motioned to him, and he walked over.

"Jabo, see the tall fellow at the bar with the Stetson on?"

"Yeah, Sylvia. I seed him a-winnin' over at the crap table."

"Well, he just walked away from the table after cleanin' out old Rufus Garrett, and I seen him upstairs sportin' a wad of hundred-dollar bills. He's loaded."

Jabo nodded and began to walk toward the back of the saloon, but Sylvia called out to him.

"Jabo, somethin' else," she whispered. "He's got a gun tucked in his belt under that jacket he's wearin'. Better watch out."

"Hell, Sylvia, they ain't no way he can take five of us."

"Don't be too sure about that, Jabo. He's a sharp fellow, and he ain't had but one drink."

"We'll see." Jabo walked to the back of the saloon and motioned to another man to follow him outside.

***

It was after midnight when Slim walked out into the clear night air, heading for the boarding houses immediately north of Jake's Place. He thought of the big lease sale, the scarlet-haired beauty he had made love to, and his good luck playing craps. It had been a great day.

"Damn, I can't believe it," he muttered. "Almost broke one minute, and now I've got almost $20,000," he mumbled. Slim continued to walk north toward his boarding house, oblivious to anything around him. It had been a perfect day, and nothing could spoil it now.

***

As Jabo, Skinner-man, Cotton, and two more of Jake's men approached a dark alley just up the street from Jake's Place. Jabo whispered to Cotton, "Cotton, don't screw this 'un up like you did last week. By God, if I hadn't whapped him with this hatchet, he'd have shot your ass off."

"Don't give me any shit, Jabo. How was I to know he weren't drunk? Damn, that asshole was as quick as a fox, but I ain't gonna let it happen with this 'un."

***

"Remember, he's tall, wearin' a Stetson and cowboy boots. Don't grab no drunk that ain't got two nickels to rub together," said Jabo.

"Yeah. Hey, I see somebody comin', and he's a tall son-of-a-bitch. Maybe that's him," Cotton whispered.

Slim had a lot on his mind as he walked down the board sidewalk. His new cowboy boots clomped along on the hollow wood boards, announcing his approach. He'd just pulled out another cigarette as he passed the alley up the street from Jake's Place. Slim was looking down to light his cigarette when Cotton, holding a piece of pipe and a knife, started toward Slim, who caught a glimpse of a figure stepping out from the shadows.

"Shit!" He jumped aside, and Cotton's lead pipe glanced off his shoulder.

"Git 'em!" yelled Jabo, and he and three other men rushed Slim.

Slim reached for his gun as Jabo and the rest of the gang rushed him. Cotton came from one side while the rest of the hijackers rushed him from the other, and in an instant Slim had made a decision. He turned his gun on the four men, and a blast from his Colt .45 sent Cal, one of Jabo's men, spinning back with a slug in his chest. However, before Slim could turn, Cotton's lead pipe hit his head, snapping it back, and he never felt Jabo's knife as it penetrated his chest.

"Damn, I thought the son-of-a-bitch was gonna kill us all," said Jabo as he kicked Slim to be sure that he was dead. "The sorry bastard got old Cal. Come on, fleece him, and let's get the hell outta here."

In a few seconds, the hijackers were pawing over Slim's lifeless body, and they quickly went through his pockets, where Jabo found a wad of bills.

"Damn, Sylvia was right again," Jabo muttered. He stuffed the bills in his pocket and grabbed one of Slim's legs. "Come here, Skinner-man. Help me pull this unlucky bastard back in the alley. Hey, wait a minute—Look at 'em brand-new boots. They looks like my size." He yanked off Slim's new boots and shoved Slim's legs off the sidewalk.

(From *The Queen of Hamburger Row*.)

***

Not only has this quarter of a block been a witness to numerous hangings and the violence of the oil boom, the buildings and alleyways adjacent to this small plot of ground have had a history of mayhem, followed by numerous paranormal occurrences. During the oil boom, crowds of men would sweep through the streets at night and vehicular traffic would halt because of the number of people in the street. A comment from Mrs. Jenson, a musician who played in the Rialto Theater orchestra, confirms this: *"We walked in the middle of the street to keep from getting hit by things and bodies thrown out upper floor windows."* (The Rialto orchestra played until the last show was over, usually around midnight. Obviously, the level of lawlessness was at its peak about this time every night.)

During the later part of the oil boom, the hastily constructed, two-story buildings that were built on the lots across from the Rialto and served as barrelhouses either burned down or were demolished to make way for studier buildings. A number of smaller brick buildings were constructed in the late 1920s and early 1930s. Then, in the early 1940s, they were remodeled and housed businesses such as a Sinclair gasoline filling station, followed by a Magnolia station in the 1950s.

Current events:

Things have changed on the lot across the street from the theater, since it became the Oil Heritage Park. And the question is: Have some of the pieces of antique oilfield equipment become a home for these wandering spirits? Is this geographical area a place for these lost spirits to congregate, or have some of the spirits from the ancient oilfields of South Arkansas followed the equipment to its present location?

Since the statues and platforms of Oil Heritage Park are located in El Dorado's entertainment district, numerous men and women stop by to read the plaques, sit on the platforms, and even climb on the statues. Over the past few years, there have been numerous reports of minor accidents in the park, most of which occurred while people were climbing on the statues or standing on the platforms.

A recurring comment from the accident victims is: *"Somebody pushed me."* Or: *"I slipped, but I don't understand why."*

Are the ghosts from past hanging from the gallows still lingering at the spot of execution? Or maybe the ghosts of the hundreds of men knifed in the adjacent alleyways are roaming the area. Have these apparitions taken up residence in the statues and other parts of the oil heritage monuments? Or did some of them simply cross the street from the old Rialto?

One thing is certain: The accounts of paranormal activities from this area cannot be explained through scientific investigation. However, psychic Carol Pate, the renowned on her walk from the train car to the Rialto Theater, did pass through the Oil Heritage Park and commented about the flashes of energy imprints and the presence of spirits. We have another visit planned for Pate, and the Oil Heritage Park is on the top of her list to be thoroughly investigated.

Recently, the area from Main Street to Cedar Street has become the center of El Dorado's Festival District, where music is preformed and, during the summer weekend, where crowds gather. As more visitors come for the music and to meet people, the number of reported incidents of paranormal activities has increased. Are the strange noises, which are sometimes heard in the nearby alleyway and around the oil heritage monuments, just normal sounds of the night? Or do these sounds come from something paranormal?

That question continues to puzzle many investigators because late at night, after everyone has departed the area, there are unusual sounds and strange sightings of lights and mists that lend credence to paranormal activities in the area. Many people think these sounds are from the ghosts of executed criminals who were hanged on the gallows. Or are they still there protesting their innocence?

One thing is certain: As the area becomes more and more popular, stories will continue to be heard about things being moved, sounds that can't be explained, and eerie mists emitting from around the statues and fother Oil Heritage Park monuments.

Some old-timers point out that the park is just adjacent to Hamburger Row, noted to be the most violent and lawless area of town. Hamburger Row was less than a block away; and hundreds of murders were documented from this area and even in the area where the Oil Heritage Park is located contributed its share of lawlessness.

These paranormal activities increased rapidly when the massive, 35-ton, antique, 1920s bull wheel and steam-driven power station were moved from Arkansas's first oilfield, the El Dorado Field, to the park. Did some of the spirits of the 1920s boom accompany the huge piece of equipment? We can't be sure, but by all accounts paranormal sounds and activities increased dramatically as soon as this piece of equipment was placed in the park.

We know there were hundreds of fatal oilfield accidents during the 1920s, because of the use of heavy equipment operated by untrained men. And in the old El Dorado Oil Field, Arkansas's first oilfield, where numerous drilling rigs punched dozens of holes around the discovery well, there are accounts of fatal-accident victims who were hurriedly buried in the mud pits associated with the drilling.

The El Dorado Oil Field produced for many years and during this time more than 50 wells were drilled. Oil-holding tanks dotted the landscape and a giant power station was constructed to provide vacuum power to pump the wells. Some 30 years ago the last well was plugged and the field was abandoned. And, as it happened many times during the early days of the oil boom, with almost no enforcement of oil and gas clean-up rules, the operators merely walked off and left the rusty tanks and equipment.

That was the case at the El Dorado Field, and when a local real estate developer purchased the land for a housing subdivision, he found, scattered in an overgrown bramble of trees and vines, the remains of the abandoned equipment. After weeks of moving hundreds of pieces of scrap metal, tanks, and other smaller pieces of equipment, only the huge, 35-ton steam-driven power station was left in the old oilfield. It took the largest crane in South Arkansas to place the 9-by-21-foot, cast-iron piece of equipment on a flatbed truck. As the massive piece of equipment was raised, several workers noted a faint puff of mist coming from the power station, and then hundreds of red wasps swarmed out to protect their home.

After this rocky start, things seemed to be under control, and the equipment was moved to a raised rack at Milam Construction to be sandblasted, repaired, and painted. After the work was complete, the equipment was loaded again and hauled to the Oil Heritage Park in downtown El Dorado.

The power station now sits on a raised platform adjacent to several bronze statues. Iron posts and cable from the abandoned El Dorado Oil Field were used to create a perimeter for the exhibit, and two planters, 4-foot in diameter, have been added as landscaping for the exhibit.

As soon as the equipment was placed in the park, there were reports of unusual activities. At night, several people commented, they could detect a glow from the old power station, and other witnesses said they heard unusual sounds, as if the motor were actually running. Several theories were postulated concerning these paranormal activities in and around the Oil Heritage Park.

Of course, since the paranormal activities increased after the massive power station was moved to the park, most people think there is a direct connection: As the ghosts from El Dorado's first oilfield migrated from one piece of equipment to the power station, which was all that remained in the abandoned oilfield, these spirits must have been in the equipment when it arrived at the park.

It seems to me that each of these theories about which spirits haunt the park have a certain amount of validity, especially the one concerning the power station, since abnormal activity increased after the equipment arrived on the scene. However, that area also has a violent and turbulent history, and many paranormal sighting and sounds were observed prior to the power station's arrival. So I have concluded that there must be more than one explanation.

Are there hosts of spirits present representing 160 years of history? Are these spirits trying to tell us something about the past that keeps them here and makes us aware of them? One day, through a psychic interpretation of their energy imprints and of their visible spirits, will we be able to hear their stories? I think the likelihood of that happening is very real, and one day, with the help of psychic interpretation, we will hear the tales of oilfield mayhem, innocent men going to the gallows, and boomtown deaths that the spirits who roam the Oil Heritage Park seem so eager to tell. But until we investigate further, and have supernatural assistance to unravel the mysteries, we can only imagine the fascinating stories these spirits have to tell.

25

THE LAST WHOREHOUSE ON HAMBURGER ROW

DURING the 1920s oil boom, brothels popped up like weeds in a neglected garden. Most of the ones within the city limits of El Dorado were in an area south of the courthouse square, primarily on Cedar Street and South Washington Avenue. Based on published information and oral history interviews, I estimate that between 20 and 30 houses of prostitution flourished in this area, which is only one block from the courthouse square.

This number may seem extraordinarily high, but in those oil-boom years, the El Dorado population increased dramatically from 3,800 to an estimated 50,000— and of that increase, some 90% were believed to be active, young males. Considering those figures, my estimate of the number of brothels is probably conservative.

Of course, that number doesn't even include the freelance prostitutes who walked the streets or the dozens of brothels in surrounding towns. Most of the active houses of prostitution were small, secondfloor hotels that allowed the girls to live there and ply their trade. (Remember that during the very early days of the boom, in 1921–1922, the brothels were gambling halls on the first floor with rooms on the second and third.)

But what is even more surprising is how long the brothels operated. According to an interview I had with the night desk clerk of the Garrett Hotel, as late as 1955, prostitutes were available in at least six hotels or boarding houses in the area. The former desk clerk noted three in the 300 block of East Cedar Street, and another three on South Washington Avenue (Hamburger Row). He picked up this information from inquires about girls made by soldiers returning from the Second World War. And actually, he missed one, which was on Main Street, almost across from First Baptist Church.

The Garrett Hotel never allowed active prostitution, but from the night desk clerk's contact with visitors who had been to the nearby brothels or hotels where prostitutes operated, he was able to accurately pinpoint every active house of prostitution.

During the 1960s, these brothels or hotels that allowed the girls to work unhindered slowly dwindled. The Randolph Hotel, for example, closed during the 1960s, when the hotel was abandoned and eventually demolished to make room for a bank parking lot. And as the active houses of prostitution closed, all that remained of old Hamburger Row were a halfdozen rundown, brick buildings, some of which would occasionally be rented for retail use.

Update: Today, the remaining buildings on South Washington Avenue consist of several substantial brick structures build in the mid-1920s. I recently interviewed one of the owners of a 1924 brick building built my Pete McCall. It was originally The Crystal Hotel, and it was a brothel from 1924 to 1974. It grabs the prize as the longest continuously operating brothel in the city—or maybe in the Mid-South.

In 2007, the citizens of El Dorado voted a one-cent sales tax to fund economic development. Part of that tax was to build a $16-million conference center to be sited on the east side of South West Avenue across from South Arkansas Junior College, two blocks from the Rialto Theater and immediately west of South Washington Avenue, (old Hamburger Row). City leaders purchased land for the conference center building and extended their purchase to include some of the remnants of Hamburger Row.

The buildings that remained were historically significant since they were part of El Dorado's 1920s history and represented the last vestiges of the oil boom. In fact, four of the remaining buildings on the north end of South Washington Avenue were the heart of old Hamburger Row, and the architects for the center recommended they be saved. However, in 2009, Mayor Mike Dumas decided to demolish these historic buildings.

The stated reason for removing the buildings was to allow for more parking behind the center. However, the conference center architects publicly stated that the extra parking space was not needed. The area with its colorful oil-boom history could have been saved and made a tourist attraction, but the area is now just an open, grassy field, with no parking, and no buildings.

It was a mistake, many believe, and wasted thousands of taxpayer dollars.

As these buildings were being demolished, however, something remarkable was uncovered. A large, wood-frame, two-story building mysteriously appeared. It was as if it had been dropped from the sky, as in The Wonderful Wizard of Oz. It seems that one of the brick buildings had encased an old wooden house, which, upon closer examination, seemed to be a small inn or hotel. Evidently, the original building was set back from the street approximately 100 feet.

I immediately began to investigate when and why the building had been constructed. From my old maps of South Arkansas, I have determined that the first railroad came into El Dorado around 1878. I have an antique map showing the first railroad under construction at that date.

In looking at the house and comparing it to the Mason House on North Jackson—which is circa1875—the mystery house on

South Washington Avenue appears to have been built sometime between 1876 and 1880. I walked through all parts of the house, except the attic, and from the layout of the rooms, it looks as if it were built as an inn, probably right after the first railroad came to El Dorado.

My walk through the house was fascinating but not without a series of strange sensations. I can only describe it as a cold dampness that seemed to penetrate, and as that wave of coldness swept over me—in the middle of a hot South Arkansas summer—the hair on the back of my neck stood straight up. But that wasn't the only thing that happened.

I checked out the rooms and one of them had a stairwell to the attic, which I started to climb. I had no sooner poked my head into the dark place than I heard something that stopped me in my tracks. It sounded as if something or somebody were scraping their fingernails on a blackboard, and then there was what I thought was a cough.

I decided I really didn't need to check out the attic.

But why was this old railroad inn hidden inside a brick building? This is what I've been able to come up with. When the 1920s oil boom began, this building was the only substantial structure on South Washington Avenue. Within a year, several rough, clapboard buildings were built on the street, and these buildings became the lawless Hamburger Row. There is no doubt in my mind, after listening to and reading the oral and written histories of the area, that this house immediately changed from a railroad inn to a barrelhouse. In fact, it was quite possibly the first saloon/gambling house/brothel in the city.

After several years of complete lawlessness on Hamburger Row, the city began to crack down and the wide-open, anything-goes atmosphere went underground. In the mid- 1920s the clapboard buildings on South Washington Avenue were torn down and brick buildings took their place. Evidently, however, this particular house must have still been a substantial structure, so the builder of the new brick building that was going up on the site, built around it, keeping a concealed entrance to the inn through what later became the kitchen at a restaurant called Joe's Place.

In order to integrate the old house into the new building, they raised the inn approximately 12 feet, so that the former ground floor became the second floor. When workers did this, they also extended the living space from the old house across the top of the new, lower building to create extra rooms. When I examined the house, I entered from the rear and walked down a wide hallway that divided the house much like a hotel hallway would. On either side of this hallway were four rooms.

Another interesting feature was located at the top of the stairs that led up from the store below. It was a small cubbyhole with a built-in desk and glass front. It was obviously used for someone to receive money and to act at as a check-in desk clerk, or, more likely, it was where the madam of the brothel held court and collected money from the girls' customers. The stairs that descended from the second floor came out in on the ground floor, through an opening cleverly concealed behind a fake wall.

As I walked through the old house, there were noises and wisps of wind that gave you an eerie feeling. As I opened a door leading to one of the rooms, I heard what I thought was someone coughing again but, of course, the room was empty. In another room, I was almost knocked over by the smell of perfume. The scent disappeared quickly, and I only smelled it that one time.

Abbreviated names and phone numbers (some only double digits) had been scribbled onto the wallpaper in one room. And although I didn't see anything I could pin down as paranormal, I sure heard and smelled plenty.

A few days after a picture of the old inn appeared in our local newspaper, I was contacted by another investigator who asserted he saw numerous orbs of energy there late one evening. He was convinced there were spirits within the old railroad inn.

Worth Camp, a local attorney said—in an e-mail, "The 1929 city directory listed 324 ½ South Washington as 'Jones Rooms'." Worth notes, "It may have had a reputation for prostitution."

Well, a reputation for prostitution was an understatement, as far as I'm concerned. I believe the building was originally constructed as an inn for railroad passengers, but when the oil boom hit, I am certain it became part of a barrelhouse that featured gambling, liquor, and prostitution. If it didn't become a barrelhouse, it would have been the only structure on Hamburger Row that wasn't

Several individuals have told me that in later years they think the building continued to be one of the houses of prostitution run by the famous El Dorado lesbian madam, Betty Fortenberry. Actually, from other interviews, I have concluded that Betty Fortenberry was very likely the owner of a number of brothels not only along South Washington Avenue, but also in villages throughout the county. From other interviews, Fortenberry has been linked with a variety of additional criminal activities. (In a later chapter, interviewers link her to the infamous Miss America robberies.)

In my interview with the former desk clerk of the Garrett Hotel, who staffed the front desk from late the late 1940s to the early 1950s, he confirmed that this the house, as well as several other buildings, such as the Randolph Hotel, were used for prostitution as late as the 1950s.

Naturally, when this house suddenly appeared, seemly out of nowhere, it became an area-wide attraction. Visitors flocked to see this strange apparition, still sitting intact on top of a 12-foot, raised foundation. It was a remarkable sight. There was an immediate move to save the house by the local historical foundation, and City Alderman Vertis Mason, from Ward One, even persuaded the mayor to delay demolition until the house could be examined.

However, the mindset in El Dorado—especially from elected officials—has been that old historic buildings are worthless and need to be demolished. And so to many people's regret, it was torn down—to make a parking lot, which was never used. The destruction of this old house eliminated one of the last, and the oldest, pieces of Hamburger Row's history.

I, myself, hated to see this house disappear. If it had been saved, it would have been a great tourist attraction to go with the conference center. I can't think of any city in the country that could boast about having an authentic, hidden whorehouse.

26

BETTY FORTENBERRY'S BLACK BOOK

OF all the characters that were a part of Hamburger Row, the red-haired, lesbian madam, Betty Fortenberry, is easily the most colorful. Her center of operations on South Washington Avenue was the upstairs Hillcrest Hotel, located in the mid-block of old Hamburger Row, and although it was a hotel with rooms to rent, most of these rooms came with a lady. Naturally, the room rates were priced accordingly because of the extra services rendered.

If even half the stories I have heard about her are true, then Fortenberry must have been quite a woman. She was "one mean bitch," as one older person described her.

Fortenberry might have been tough as nails, but she was also an astute businesswoman. Her various businesses were run with remarkable precision, and she kept a record of everything. She has been linked to not just one, but a string of brothels, and even though she is usually thought of as being the leading madam of Hamburger Row, her other activities included brothels in other parts of Union County, specifically around the Smackover Field. She was also involved in several legitimate businesses in the county, and in every business, she kept detailed records.

Just the thought of everything that happened in her brothels being recorded with names, dates, and activity has caused many South Arkansas residents and former residents to lose sleep. According to several sources, she kept a personal "little black book" that had the name of every customer who walked into her establishments. And the book included not only the client's name, but his preference for the type of sex he enjoyed, and his choice of girls.

It was all officially noted, and, according to one account, Fortenberry bragged that the little black book was her "get-out-of-jail-free" ticket. In a recent conversation with a retired Union County judge, he confirmed that Fortenberry did indeed keep a little black book detailing her activities. Evidently, it was common knowledge (as per conversations with elderly citizens) that she kept the record book.

When I first heard of Fortneberry's alleged little back record book, which listed all of the customers of her whorehouses, I thought of the Hollywood madam who scandalized Southern California by revealing some of the names of her regulars. Evidently, Betty Fortneberry's records were also very detailed and embarrassing.

Just think for a moment about a little black book with page after page of names, amounts, and notations linking some of the most prosperous and influential people in South Arkansas to brothels, as well as specific girls and what types of sex they preferred. And, of course, as every good businessperson would do, Fortenberry made a record of how much each man paid and what he tipped.

There are numerous accounts from girls who worked for Fortenberry that collaborate the stories of how she kept meticulous records. According to these girls, they were instructed to keep an exact record of all the men they entertained, including each full name and address, the day and hour they were with him, and the amount he paid. After a night's work, each girl would sit down with the madam and recount from their notes, exactly every encounter they'd had. Fortenberry would list, under each girl's name, the customer, his address, and other pertinent information.

Well, according to many sources, such a book certainly existed or maybe still exists. And, these same sources say, that juicy little manuscript would be a shocking revelation to many families in town. It seems that this most interesting diary had not only names and address but also vivid descriptions of the interactions with girls that took place in Fortneberry's various establishments. It also contained notes out by the side of each man listed his choice of girls and his sexual preferences.

In addition to this list of customers, there is supposedly also a record of money paid by each man. Fortenberry also recorded the transfer of girls to various other South Arkansas and Mississippi towns, along with the dates and amounts charged for their transportation. Other, little-black-book entries reportedly detailed every payment made to law enforcement officials.

It has long been rumored that the brothels of the 1920s, which seemed exempt from the law, must have had an arrangement with the authorities to assure that the law would not bother their businesses. After all, how on earth could multiple prostitution rings, which even schoolboys knew about, be kept secret from the police and sheriff's office? The sheriff's office was only a block away, and city hall was only two blocks. What arrangements did Betty Fortenberry have with the local law enforcement officers, and what about the city council and mayor—not to mention the bankers, lawyers, church leaders, and other businessmen who winked at the practice?

Well, evidently the powerful madam knew she had something that she could someday use, and it's rumored that in the early 1960s she used her little black book to avoid being charged for directing as many as 10 robberies that occurred in one day. (Details are in the next chapter, *The Miss America Robberies.*)

Betty Fortenberry retired—or as one informant told me, "jumped bail"—shortly before the Randolph Hotel closed, and, according to one of her friends, she made several comments about the book, indicating it might fund her retirement.

It has been 50 years since Fortenberry left town, and although many prominent names have been bandied about—as if they were quotes from some unnamed source—the little black book has never been made public. Will it surface from the belongings of someone in one of the nursing homes one day to reveal the activities of hundreds of El Dorado's finest? Will some of the revelations having to do with law enforcement shock the readers? We can only speculate about the book's content, but from several sources, we know there was indeed a record kept of some of the most notorious activities in Union County history. Did Fortenberry sell the book and retire with the proceeds, as she had indicated to some of her friends? Or did she keep it with her and one day it will surface and its contents will be displayed for all to see. Most items such as this will one day appear. It seems the people who own such things can't bear to destroy them. It will be a very revealing day when we get a firsthand look at the underbelly of Hamburger Row, or, I might say, what went on under the sheets by El Dorado's elite. Recently, I interviewed an elderly gentlemen who was well into his 90s. I have agreed not to use his name but he came to El Dorado when he was a young boy. His family lived very near the downtown, and he witnessed many of the early lawless years of the oil boom. His stories about several events I mentioned in the preceding chapters are remarkably similar to other accounts, and two of his stories were particularly revealing.

One narrative was about a Dr. White, who maintained an office on the ground floor of the downtown Armstrong Building across from the courthouse. It seems, based on my interview with this unnamed source, that Dr. White was associated in some way with Betty Fortenberry.

According to this eyewitness, Dr. White routinely left his office unlocked on Friday and Monday nights, and after 6 p.m. on those nights, several carloads of women would arrive and enter the office. There were four examining rooms, and soon the women had spread out and occupied them all. Minutes later, dozens of men began to arrive, and soon these "ladies of the night" were doing a booming business.

Of course, since these women were "working" less than a half-mile down the street, why didn't their customers go to them? The answer is relatively simple; The customers, knowing the after-dark dangers associated with Hamburger Row, were very reluctant to even walk down Hamburger Row after dark. The courthouse square where the Armstrong Building is located, was a much safer place since it was right across the street from the sheriff's office in the courthouse and police station a block away.

Yes, it's pretty obvious that these customers knew they wouldn't be bothered by law enforcement officials.

The owners of the Armstrong Building tried—unsuccessfully—to get Dr. White to lock his office at night, but he said, **"Work in the oilfields goes on 24 hours a day, and I want to have my office available in case of an accident. The women you saw going in were probably nurses."**

Well, it's not recorded what the response was to the doctor's ridiculous statement, but Dr. White didn't stop leaving his office doors unlocked. Naturally, he was never seen going by his office after hours to minister to any injured oilfield workers.

The idea of bringing the girls to the customers was increasingly common as the number of drilling rigs increased and the male population swelled. Since drilling an oil well is a 24-hour-a-day job, and many crews were shorthanded, a driller or floor-hand might end up staying on a drilling rig for several weeks at a time, sleeping in a tent beside the rig.

Naturally, for men confined to a remote location away from the barrelhouses on Hamburger Row, there was a pent-up desire for something to do in order to alleviate the boredom. Several of the barrelhouse owners quickly figured out a way to take advantage of this potential business, and, naturally, make a little extra money.

If the drilling rig was operating in a known field, such as the Smackover Field (where several drilling rigs were operating in close proximity), the barrelhouse owner would bring his girls out to the field, and set up a large circus-like tent where he could serve drinks and furnish women to the crews. If the weather was good, his girls could stay overnight. However, if the drilling was on a wildcat, at a remote location, it was common practice to have the girls ride up on horseback.

The following in an excerpt from *The Queen of Hamburger Row*. This fictional account will give you an idea of how the appearance of a couple of girls riding up to a drilling rig on horseback might have looked.

> …and he was still shaking his head in disbelief when he heard a woman's voice.
>
> "Hi, boys."
>
> Everyone turned around to see a woman on horseback not 20 yards away, closely followed by a second woman. Since the drill-site was at least eight miles from El Dorado, Bill shook his head in wonder as they rode up. They were young girls, no older than 20, with stringy, short, blonde hair. Their faces were dripping with sweat from the eight-mile ride, and they were riding Western style, wearing low-cut blouses and flared skirts. Bill knew immediately that these weren't farm girls out for a ride.

"Oh, damn! Get the hell out of here!" Hays yelled. "You damn whores!"

"Shut up, Hays! You ain't the king of these here woods! We got as much right to be out here as you do!" yelled one of the women.

"Hays, do you know these women?" asked Bill.

"Yeah, they work down at Silvertop's barrelhouse, and that worthless piece of thrash sends 'em out to the rigs on horseback every Saturday. I've, uh, well, talked with both of them several times, but shit, they need to keep away from where men are workin' and do their foolin' around' back at Silvertop's place."

"You mean…" said Clyde.

"Yeah, for five bucks they'll take you out in the woods and service you."

"Well, I'll be damned."

By this time, the women had ridden up to the rig and were waving at the driller and the three floor-hands, who had walked over the edge of the rig floor and were trying to hear the women over the roar of the drilling rig motors.

The driller went over and kicked the kelly out of gear and set the brake. In a few seconds, the four-man crew had left the rig and were heading for the women.

"Wait a minute!" screamed Hays. "Get your asses back on the floor, and leave them whores alone!"

Three of the crewmen ignored Hays, and soon they were standing by the two women, laughing and talking, but Bud, the driller, walked over to where Hays and Clyde's crew were standing.

"Listen, Hays, we ain't gonna be long, and if we don't get to be with them women, it'll probably take longer to drill this dry hole. And who knows? One of 'em hands is liable to get careless and drop a wrench in the hole. God, I'd hate that, wouldn't you?"

"Oh, my God!" yelled Hays in frustration.

Hays stood there fuming, but finally agreed. "Okay, go ahead, but if y'all ain't back to drillin' in an hour, I'm gonna dock your pay a dollar."

Bud smiled and walked over to where one of the men was in the progress of negotiating a price for the whole crew. One of the girls pulled down her top and yelled, "This here's a free peek, but the rest is gonna cost ya." Finally Bill heard somebody yell, "Twenty dollars, and that's our final offer!"

One of the women smiled and reached her hand out to Bud.

"Come on, big boy, you can be first." She motioned for him to hop on the horse behind her. He jumped on the back of her saddle and they headed for the woods. Another member of the rig crew climbed on behind the other woman and followed them while the rest of the crew waited.

"Shit, let's go back to town, boys, 'cause ain't no drillin' gonna happen around for the next hour or so," said Hays.

[From *The Queen of Hamburger Row*]

27

THE MISS AMERICA ROBBERIES

IN 1964, El Dorado native Donna Axum was named Miss America. Back in the decades from the 1940s to the mid-90s Miss America was a huge honor, and for a small Southern town to have one of their own named was overwhelming.

Every person who hailed from El Dorado or who was then living in El Dorado could tell you exactly where they were when Donna was named Miss America. For a week, it was the talk of the town, and then the town began to prepare for Donna's return with a welcome-home parade and dinner. However, according to my interviews, the parade and dinner drew the attention of someone else in town, who made plans that had nothing to do with the celebration.

The anticipated turnout for the parade and dinner was expected to be huge, and, of course, every prominent family in town was involved in some way. Naturally, these families were the same ones who profited from the 1920s oil boom, and they represented most of the wealth in the community.

In my interviews and discussions, I have recorded two accounts of what came to be rumored as the Miss America Robberies. Both of the stories involved Betty Fortenberry and the robbery of one or more prominent family homes during the festivities.

According to one source, the night after the big homecoming parade for El Dorado's Miss America, Donna Axum, there was an exclusive dinner in the Petroleum Club located on the second floor of the Randolph Hotel. During that dinner, according to the man I interviewed, Betty Fortenberry engineered a robbery of Miss America's father's home. Evidently, the man who did the robbery took everything portable in sight and then carried it all down to one of Fortneberry's brothels on South Washington Avenue. When the madam examined what he had stolen, she actually made him return with the pieces that had little value. (Evidently, the man was an amateur crook, and did not know silver-plate from sterling silver.)

Within a few days, the thief was apprehended and implicated Fortenberry, who was arrested. My source confirms her arrest, and said Dr. White put up her bail of $50,000. A few days later, Fortenberry disappeared, skipped bail, and reportedly fled to Tennessee, where El Dorado's legendary red-haired, lesbian madam, married, raised a family, and retired from the world's oldest profession.

Dr. White was out $50,000 and later came under investigation by the State of Arkansas. His license to practice medicine was eventually revoked.

A few years later, Fortneberry's property was sold in a tax sale, and during the clean-up of the premises, the buyer found a few pages of the madam's accounts receivable book. Evidently, it was a notated ledger, but not the rumored little black book. There were many names of prominent citizens in the ledger, and one courthouse official had so many charges for his time with various girls that this man's hundreds of visits to a house of ill repute became a running joke in town.

Other items were found in the building during its clean-up, including receipt for a round, red-velvet bed and 6-inch-thick carpet. (It's likely that these notes were part of the daily record that Fortenberry kept, and were later detailed in her little black book.)

[A similar, but slightly different, story about the rumored Miss America Robberies.]

Another one of my sources, also stated that Fortenberry was involved in the Miss America Robberies, but this person's story differs in several ways from the first account. Of course, on that day of special recognition, Donna received the keys to the city, but the big event was the parade honoring her. That afternoon at 2 o'clock, virtually every soul in Union County lined Main Street to watch the parade featuring their own Miss America. It was the most publicized activity honoring Donna Axum, and the parade boasted the highest attendance of any event in the city's history. The story below is one man's recollection of what happened during the parade:

The Miss America Robberies involved more than one home, and all of the robberies took place during the time the parade was held, instead of the dinner, said my source. Since the entire El Dorado Police force was patrolling the parade, and virtually the entire town was lined up along the parade route, it seemed like a perfect time to rob a number of prominent family homes, including the Axums'.

So, while the town's most prominent and wealthy citizens were feting Miss America, Fortenberry reportedly had more sinister things in mind. It was a time before alarm systems were routinely installed in homes, and in many small Southern towns, most homeowners didn't even lock their doors. The entire police force and fire department had also accompanied Miss America on the parade route, leaving the city without any law enforcement officials on duty.

According to my unnamed source, at exactly 2 o'clock a number of men began to rob the homes of the wealthiest families in town. The parade, dedication, and speech by various dignitaries took well over two hours. When these families returned to their homes, they found them ransacked. Hundreds of pieces of antique silver were stolen, as well as jewelry, china, and even fur coats.

Of course, you would expect a series of robberies of this magnitude would be front-page news in every paper in the state. But, remember, residents had made it a practice to promote an image of a quiet, peaceful town, and not only was there no widespread newspaper publicity, the alleged, multiple robberies didn't even rate a spot in the local paper.

The thefts were whispered talk at cocktail parties, and fingers were pointed at Betty Fortenberry. However, even though the madam was arrested, she was never charged with any crime and was released almost as soon as she reached the courthouse, according to my sources. Was she released on bail, or because of other reasons?

If there were a series of robberies, why were they not recorded by the local police? Many think they were ignored, and some go as far to say they are certain of it. If that's true, then why weren't any of the robberies reported? Did Fortenberry hold some incriminating evidence that she threatened to use against the law, or did she threaten to reveal some of the names in her little black book?

We can only guess, but such widespread speculation as to why the robberies weren't reported must have some foundation. The most obvious reason for a cover-up, of course, is that any prosecution of Betty Fortenberry might prompt her to reveal some very embarrassing information: one, that some of the leading citizens of the community had paid for services of prostitutes at the Randolph Hotel and other brothels on South Washington Avenue; and, second, that the law enforcement community knew about it for years—but did nothing. Therefore, it seems logical that Fortneberry's gang could rob more than a dozen houses and steal thousands of dollars with impunity.

There's another story about the Miss America Robberies that has been repeated many times. It seems that after the incident, a man was apprehended trying to hock some silver items that were stolen in one of the robberies. He was taken to the police station and, after being threatened with life in prison, he confessed that he was part of the robberies, but only a small part. The following is a guess at what might have happened.

"Chief, I'm just a small fish. Them others is the ones that planned it and got folks like me to do the job."

"Who did the planning and who hired you?"

"Betty Fortenberry."

"Are you sure?"

"Yes, she's the one who planed everything and even told me which house I was to rob. Now, Chief, you promised me a light sentence if I confessed and told you who done did it."

"Yeah, we'll take care of you, but you've got to testify in court that Betty hired you."

"Okay, but I need protection, if I get out on bail."

"You ain't gonna get no bail until I get Betty behind bars."

"Dawson, swear out an arrest warrant for Betty Fortenberry and bring her to my office."

An hour later, Betty Fortenberry was ushered into the chief's office.

"Sit down, Betty, we got some talking to do."

"Damn, Chief, what's the idea of dragging me up to the station? If your men need a little something extra, you could have just sent one of them down to my place, and I'd have taken care of 'em."

"This ain't about your business, Betty. Listen, I told you to just keep your head down and you wouldn't have any trouble out of us, but, hell, robbing half the town ain't keeping your head down. You have really screwed up, and I ain't got no choice but to arrest you."

"Hell, Chief, you can arrest me but you need some evidence. Hearsay ain't good enough."

"I got Billy Jack Tauton, and he's agreed to testify against you. Hell, he's gonna say you was the brains behind all them robberies, and even told him which houses to rob."

Betty took a deep breath, reached over and picked up the Chief's writing pad and wrote down several names.

"What the hell are you doing?"

"I'm just putting down a list of men I'm gonna use as character references."

"Let me see that list—shit, Betty, these men are the backbone of this town. You can't have them testify on your behalf. They don't even know you."

"The hell they don't!"

"What?"

"Here, I keep a couple of pages that I've copied out of my little black book just in case I need a little help getting out a tight spot—take a look at these pages."

The chief flipped through the several pages, and as he did he understood what he was reading.

"Surely to God, you ain't gonna make this public!"

"Why, no, Chief, I don't plan to, but just remember this is only a copy of three pages of a little black book that is two inches thick. There's names, girls, and prices from the 1920s right up to last week, and some of your boys are on almost every page—'course they are marked as free. Naw, I ain't gonna make this public—unless I have to."

"Listen to me, Betty. I've got enough evidence to send you to Tucker Prison for life."

"Oh, send me to a woman's prison? Hell, Chief, go ahead and throw me in that briar patch!"

"Damn it, Betty, you can't rob half the town and expect me to let you walk out of here without doing anything."

"Chief, let's quit bullshitting each other. You know they's no way in hell the men in my little black book will stand for that stuff to hit the paper. They'll be all over your ass for letting it out. So, let me get back to my business, and I'll forget all about using my little black book for character references."

"Oh, my God, Betty!—Get out of my office!"

Well, my take on the above stories is this: I think there is a good possibility that because of the opportunity that presented itself during the time Miss America was feted, some robberies were committed. And Betty Fortenberry could easily have been involved. However, the story that has multiple robberies occurring, including one at the home of Miss America's parents, is difficult to believe. My mother was Miss America's chaperone during the Miss America Pageant, and she was with Donna continually during the time she was honored in El Dorado. Donna never mentioned anything about her parents' home being burglarized.

However, the elderly person who recounted the robberies is a reputable source, and he told the story as fact—not rumor.

28

VARIOUS ENCOUNTERS

EL Dorado seems to have ghosts in every nook and cranny. As I was compiling this book, several people contacted me about paranormal experiences they'd had in or around the city. I have included several especially interesting ones. In fact, one of the men I interviewed believes the area extending out from the center of town for at least a mile is home to numerous spirits, and he's had a paranormal encounters to prove his theory.

After I finished my investigation in the downtown area, I became certain that spirits are present in almost every old downtown building, and from some of the comments I have heard, it seems they are not confined to downtown El Dorado. To make my investigation complete, I have included several of these paranormal experiences from farther afield. The first is from **Montana Staples, age 10.**

"I have a story that happened to me when I was nine years old at Mr. Vergil Amason's funeral at Bethel Cemetery. After the preacher gave his announcements, I happened to glance over at three black men floating in thin air. One had a pipe and real fancy clothing, just sitting in the air. The other two also had fancy clothing on, standing in the air. At first, I thought they were the men who were going to bury the body. So I looked over to the other side of the field and realized they were not. They looked like rich men in 1950s outfits.

"I felt chill bumps all over my body! I asked Barbra Nelson (who was there with me) if she saw what was out in the field. She said she couldn't see anything but open ground. Right then and there I knew they were ghosts. When we were leaving, I didn't see them anywhere! It was spooky!

"P. S. Now, I'm ten years old."

"Sincerely,
Montana Staples"

***

The Handprint

Here's the story of a strange handprint: It seems, in a house adjacent to downtown El Dorado, a hall tree—one used for hanging hats, umbrellas, and coats—all of a sudden exhibited a mysterious handprint. It was obvious enough to notice as one walked by, and, of course, the lady of the house, upon spotting it, went right to work in removing it.

With just a wipe the handprint was gone—at least until the next day, when it appeared again. This time a determined lady set about to scrub and wash the hall tree and stepped back to admire her work. She had done such a good job that the finish was almost removed from the front of the piece.

However, the next day the handprint reappeared again. Determination set in and finally, after the hall tree was stripped and restrained, the handprint, it seemed, was gone for good. However, less than a week later, it reappeared. Then the unsettled family had been through enough, and they hauled the hall tree off to an antique store and sold it. It has since disappeared, but somewhere, probably in El Dorado, there is an old hall tree with a mysterious handprint on the front.

The Spirits of St. Mary's

On Nov. 20, 2012, at 8:30 a.m., the St. Mary's Episcopal Morning Prayer group was meeting for Morning Prayer. The church was empty and the doors were locked, except for the door to the chapel where the prayer group had gathered. During the quiet time, prior to the start of the formal prayer service, all four members of the prayer group heard footsteps in the sanctuary adjoining the chapel. Everyone in the group heard the footsteps, and when the service was over, they all commented about them. No one had been in the church and the doors were still locked. Were these steps similar to the sounds of steps commonly heard in the Rialto Theater as spirits make themselves known? Yes, I think there is a very likely connection, but not with the Rialto spirits. Adjacent to the sanctuary, on the east side of the church, is a prayer garden where there is a repository for the ashes of many former church members. I believe the spirits from the former members are making themselves known. There is no other logical conclusion.

The Main Street Antique Mall Building

This old 1920s structure is a massive, four-story, brick building on Main Street, a former furniture store. The interior of the building has its original tin ceilings and it is currently being used as an Antique Mall. I interviewed three ladies who work there and their stories are very interesting. After I finished the interview, I was sure El Dorado has another haunted building in its downtown.

It seems, from the number of paranormal sounds that have been reported during my interviews, the spirits that reside in a place have several ways of making themselves known. Very obvious footsteps coming from an area where no one can possibly be is one of their favorite ways to announce that someone is not alone. In this building, the sound of footsteps on the third and fourth floors has been so obvious that numerous individuals have reported it. It occurs when the stairwell doors are locked, and when it is impossible for anyone to be on the third or fourth floor.

Another common way for the spirits to announce themselves is to release a scent. In the Rialto Theater, smelling a cigar or perfume is one of the most common of the paranormal experiences. This paranormal visitation is also present in the Antique Mall Building. All three of the ladies I intervened noted smelling what they called Youth-Dew, a spicy perfume by Estée Lauder, introduced in 1953. And they also noted the smell of an old pipe, a cigar, and Juicy Fruit Gum.

However, the most dramatic paranormal occurrence was what the ladies called "Fairy Dust," a sparkling orb of flashing, reflective matter that was sighted in several places in the building, and, on one occasion, was seen by a customer. That customer pointed to a ball of flashing bits of something floating over the door.

"What is that?" she remarked as the other ladies watched in amazement and the orb slowly disappeared.

One of the ladies is a young, active woman, who noted that she never stumbles while at home, in any stores or on walks over El Dorado's broken sidewalks. However, when she is in the Antique Mall, she stumbles frequently. The floor is perfectly smooth, without any carpet of other material that might cause her to trip. She is sure something else is involved.

After my interview, I was certain that the building is haunted by several spirits.

The Elm Street Bakery

Across the square from the courthouse, on the corner of Elm Street and Jefferson Avenue, is the Elm Street Bakery. It one of the older buildings in the downtown, built around 1910 and remodeled during the oil boom of the 1920s. Numerous incidents have convinced the owner of the bakery that one or more spirits are making themselves known.

The building is a two-stroy brick building with an original 1920s tin ceiling and hanging light fixtures with ceiling fans. One of more unusual paranormal incidents happened to one of the lighted fans.

For a number of months, one of the brass strings used to adjust the fan speed up or down, for no apparent reason, would occasionally swing out and make a ting on one of the light globes. The lady who opened the bakery each morning got in the habit of smiling and saying, "Good morning, Mr. Hall." (Author's note: The bakery building was, for many years, the site of Hall Pharmacy.)

However, after a few weeks, for some reason, the tingling sound against the light globe stopped.

For about a month nothing happened. Then one day the lady who owned the bakery was telling someone about the strange way the fixture was sometimes hit by the brass string. Then she said, "Well, whatever caused it is not here anymore." Those words were no more than out of her mouth when the light fixture globe that had been tinged came loose from its holder and flew across the room. Evidently, the spirit wanted to let the owner know it was still around!

Another paranormal sighing occurred while one of the workers was setting up the salad bar for lunch. She heard steps, turned around, and saw a man walking up some back stairs. But as she moved to get a better look to see who it was, he disappeared. The stairs led to a sealed-off upper floor.

However, the moving clock stories seem to be the most interesting of all the tales of paranormal experiences in the bakery. The bakery owner has a large, round face clock with a strap on the back for hanging. At first, she hung it over the sink in the kitchen only to find it the next day halfway across the room. She moved it to another location only to find it on the floor. The hook she hung the clock on was still in the wall, but the clock was on the floor. And there was another time when she was in another room, heard something crash, and walked into the kitchen to find the clock all the way across the room.

Of course, many spirits who want to make themselves known, produce the sound of someone walking, and the workers in Elm Street Bakery have heard numerous sounds of someone walking up the stairs or in the hall upstairs.

Yes, the owner of the bakery believes the building is haunted, and after talking with her, I agree. The Elm Street Bakery is haunted by several spirits.

The Old Bank of Commerce Building (current offices of Gibraltar Energy)

The old Bank of Commerce Building is one of the few downtown buildings that predates the 1920s oil boom. This two-story, red-brick building, now on the National Register of Historic Places, was constructed in 1916, and until the early 1970s served as the home of the National Bank of Commerce. During this time, the bank occupied primarily the first floor and various business offices were on the second floor of the building. At one time, for example, two dentists had offices there and during the oil boom, several oil-related business were located on the upper floor.

In 1978, I purchased the building and remodeled it into offices for Gibraltar Energy, which still occupies the entire building. Over the years, only creaks and normal sounds have been heard in the building, but during the last year or so that changed. The office manager and accountant, Susan Barnett, works flex hours, and frequently comes in very early in the morning—sometimes before 6 am.

On the first floor, there is a door between the foyer and the offices in the middle and back of the building. It is a solid door, and when it is closed it makes a distinctive sound echoing through the building. Ms. Barnett, when she is in her office with all the doors in the building still locked, has noted the door slamming several times, when it was physically impossible for anyone to be in the building or for the wind to blow the door shut.

During my investigation into the downtown area, I have determined that spirits frequently make themselves known by sounds, smells, or, occasionally, by sight. The shutting of doors, especially in the Rialto Theater, is one of the most common spirit indicators. I believe the door shutting in the old Bank of Commerce Building is also an example of a spirit making itself known.

As far as I know, there have not been any tragedies associated with this building, but considering it was a bank and assorted offices for nearly a 100 years, it wouldn't surprise me if there is something in its past that has caused a spirit to occupy the building.

However, a slamming door is not the only paranormal occurrence that has been noted. I have a CD—clock radio behind my desk. I rarely play it. However, within the past few months, I have walked into my office and heard the radio playing. At first, I thought someone had turned it on and neglected to turn it off, but no one in our organization had even been in my office.

When it first happened, I would merely walk over and turn it off. However, last week, just as I was about to finish this manuscript, the radio playing moved to a new level. I walked in on Monday morning as usual and the radio was on. Before turning it off, I walked back to tell my office manager that it was on, but suddenly it went off. There is no way for this piece of electronic equipment to act on its own. Nothing was set, and there has never been a blip in its operation.

The Eyes

About a mile from downtown El Dorado, a north-south county road meanders across the outskirts of town. It connects highway 82 with highway 7. This story, told by Roy Lee McAdams of El Dorado, has to do with a strange sighting that took place just off the road from Ebenezer Baptist Church.

An old cemetery road leaves the main road, and goes less than a mile south to a small, abandoned cemetery. McAdams tells a story that happened a number of years ago, but to him it is just a vivid as if it had happened yesterday.

It seems that stories of something being seen or heard near the old cemetery had become a matter of small-town gossip. Curiosity got the best of four young men, and they decided to drive out late one night to the cemetery and see if they could see or hear anything. They arrived at the cemetery, got out of the car, and proceeded to watch and listen. In a few minutes, they heard something moving in the brush 30 or 40 yards away from the car. It started toward them and, according to their account, they could see two glowing eyes that were at least 10 inches apart.

One of the young men broke and ran all the way back to the main road. The other three stayed, mesmerized, and as they listened and watched, the two glowing eyes floated closer and closer. They were right in front of the car when one of the group said, "Quick, turn on the car lights!"

In a few seconds, the car headlights were shining out to where the glowing eyes had last been seen, but there was nothing there and they didn't hear another sound. However, the eyewitnesses all recounted the same thing, and to this day, they are convinced that a very large being—or something simulating a very large person or animal—was out there.

HealthWorks Fitness Center

HealthWorks is located on the edge of downtown El Dorado, less than two blocks from the courthouse square. It occupies the site of several much-older buildings that were taken down in order to build the best fitness center in the Mid-South.

The center has been in operation for several years, and, according to the instructors and management who operate the facility, no one had noticed anything out of the ordinarily—that is until a few weeks back when a series of incidents suddenly occurred: Lights came on in locked rooms, and equipment was moved when the building was empty.

As these events became more and more numerous, the instructors were determined to find the cause. They eliminated the human factor—by locking up equipment areas and unused rooms—and then they became convinced that something paranormal was occurring. And while there have not been any sounds, smells, or sightings in the building, they are sure something or someone is trying to make itself known.

Union County Courthouse

A block north of the Rialto Theater stands the largest and most impressive courthouse in Arkansas. After the money from the oil boom washed over South Arkansas, citizens of Union Country decided the old redbrick Victorian courthouse was too small, and they commissioned a new courthouse to be built on the same tract of land. The old courthouse was torn down and in 1928 a new courthouse was dedicated. It was, and still is, the premier facility of its kind in the state.

Up until 10 years ago the upper floor served as the county, jail with an adjoining apartment that at one time housed the jailer and his family. The basement of the building supposedly had the entrance or, depending on which way you are traveling, the exit of the Rialto–Courthouse Tunnel.

Today there is no trace of the rumored tunnel. A solid plaster wall across the south wall of the basement hides the tunnel entrance. That is if there was a tunnel.

Because of the potential to delve into the paranormal occurrences and energy imprints, we have reserved an afternoon for Ms. Pate, the psychic, to visit the building.However, my preliminary investigation confirms that the courthouse is haunted, specifically the old apartment upstairs. Longtime employees of the county have reported numerous sounds and indications of paranormal activity, and it is obvious there are one or more spirits residing in the building.

I am certain when our investigation is complete, there will be numerous other indications of spirit activity.

29

MY EXPERIENCE

ALTHOUGH I have a record of many accounts about paranormal occurrences in the Rialto Theater, as well as other strange events that have occurred in the vicinity, I had never heard or seen anything that I would call unusual until recently.

That all changed on Tuesday afternoon, May 25, 2010, at about 2 p. m. Earlier that day I had a call from Mark Givens, El Dorado's Main Street Director. He requested some new photos of the interior of the Rialto Theater in order to add them to an application for a renovation grant. I took my camera and strolled down to the theater, turned on all the lights, locked the door behind me, and proceeded to take pictures.

In order to show the new lights that had been added to the theater, I went up onto the stage and began to photograph two new rows of lights, which had just been installed.

The old theater was built in 1916, enlarged in 1925, and expanded in 1929 to become the new Rialto—our present-day theater. From its beginning, the theater was designed to be a live-performance venue as well as a movie theater. The stage-area ceiling is some 70 feet above the stage and the movie screen is attached to cables where it can be raised and lowered to allow live performances.

During our latest renovation, we decided to temporarily return the stage to its vaudeville appearance by raising the screen into the fly space. Our contractor climbed to the top of the fly space where a wooden catwalk extends across the back wall. While he was there, the contractor found the original, padded, hanging drapes from 1929 that were used when the theater first opened and the sound was too harsh. Several of these drapes, which will be used in the final restoration of the theater, have decorative stenciling and fringe in good condition.

The first of two paranormal occurrences happened when I was standing in the middle of the stage trying to photograph the row of stage lights right above me. The stage lights hang some 25 feet above the stage, and shine down. Above the stage between the catwalk and the hanging lights, there are no lights—only darkness, and a catwalk some 70 feet above the stage against the back wall.

As I stood there, all of a sudden I heard heavy footsteps coming from the dark area above the stage. Someone or something was walking, and then running, on the catwalk. I dismissed it as an animal, but in a few seconds, the sounds continued. Then I realized the heavy steps were much too loud and strong to be any kind of an animal.

The steps would stop for a few seconds and then start again as if someone were walking back and forth on the catwalk. I was certain the sounds I heard came from the catwalk, and as I stood there the hair on the back of my neck rose.

Then, as quickly as the steps started, they stopped. I had a small flashlight that I tried to shine up toward the catwalk, but it was much too small. I took a few more photos and then left the stage and began to walk toward the front of the theater to leave.

As I took that simple walk up the right aisle of the main auditorium, I had another paranormal experience. I had walked about halfway up the aisle when it was as if I had walked into a room where someone was smoking a cigar. It was unmistakably the odor of cigar smoke.

Well, I took another deep breath and continued up toward the front of the theater, and just as I was about to push open one of the doors I thought I heard laughter. It might not have been actual laugher, but it seemed as if it were.

Later, I tried to envision what could have caused the sounds I heard and the scent of a cigar I smelled, but I couldn't come up with anything that would account for them. Then, as I remembered the old theater manager from the 1940s and '50s, Mr. Robb, I thought about his ever-present cigar.

Was it the spirit of the ever-present Mr. Robb, who always stood in the lobby or on the first-stair landing letting me know he was still watching over his theater? I can only say this: There are numerous documented occurrences where individuals have smelled cigar smoke in the Rialto. Some incidences have been reported in the lobby, others upstairs on the mezzanine. Now I can add my own experience.

Yes, I think the only explanation is that Mr. Robb is one of the ghosts of the Rialto. After all Ms. Pate, the psychic, described him perfectly when she visited the theater—right down to his stubby cigar.

But what about the walking on the catwalk above the stage? It seems to me, from my investigation, that different ghosts give different signals of their presence. With Mr. Robb, it's the smell of his cigar. Maybe the walking on the catwalk is a ghost from the construction days of the theater when men were killed plunging from the upper scaffolding, and maybe the laughter is from yet another spirit.

Another signal from a different ghost is the sighting of a woman wearing vintage clothing. She is always seen in or around the Lady's Rest room. Ms. Pate says she is a blonde woman who seems to be in great distress, rushing in and out of the rest room. Could this spirit be from one of the women who were killed in the balcony? Or could the spirit be from the woman who fell from over the balcony rail onto the concrete floor of the main auditorium? Or maybe it is the ghost of a vaudeville actress from the pre-movie era, a ghost who is in costume?

Hearing someone walking in various parts of the theater is one of the most common paranormal happenings that have been reported. Many times footsteps have been heard going up and down the stairs. The logical conclusion is that it is Mr. Richardson, the old projectionist from the '40s through the '60s, making his rounds as a handyman.

Ms. Pate said the most prevalent of the spirits she encountered was a man who fits the description of Mr. Richardson. She said he was not only a projectionist, but also a handyman around the theater. He had even lived in the theater, according to Ms. Pate. And that is exactly what Mr. Richardson did for many years.

Ms. Pate also said he seems a little grouchy and very possessive of the theater. When she tried to go into the projection booth, he told her, *"You don't belong here! Get out!"*

It seems to me that putting all of the stories together confirms that the Rialto Theater is the home to multiple ghosts, spirits, and energy imprints, and these numerous spirits want to make themselves known.

30

CONCLUSION

AFTER studying the rumors and legends, and after researching the tragic and lawless history of El Dorado, I have concluded that the 10 blocks of downtown El Dorado have seen a variety of tragic and horrific events, which include hangings, gunfights, knifings, and even the desecration of a cemetery. It is no wonder that paranormal occurrences in El Dorado are common.

When you consider all the historic events and combine them with the documented paranormal experiences, you cannot help but conclude that the violent history of this community and its incidents of paranormal experiences are related. In fact, it is my opinion that it is because of this horrific history that so many spirits reside here. In other words, the spirits are here only because of the tragic events that make up the history of this town.

Can it be that these spirits, who seem to be everywhere in downtown El Dorado, are making themselves known for some reason? Could it be because of the tragic deaths so many people? And could these spirits be crying out for justice that never occurred?

We may never know, but it seems to me that the connection between violence and paranormal occurrences is overwhelming.

The Rialto Theater, The Crystal Hotel, Oil Heritage Park, the Main Street Antiques Building, Elm Street Bakery, La Piazza Restaurant, the 1878 Central of Georgia Coach, the old Bank of Commerce Building, and rooms in Union Square Guest Quarters—all have been the scenes of paranormal experiences, which multiple individuals have recounted. I believe these paranormal events have a common thread. Because of the violent history of this town, which includes so many tragic deaths, a concentration of spirits inhabits this small South Arkansas village, and each place that has a spirit presence has a past that is the site of some heinous crime.

Perhaps it is the circumstance surrounding the death of an individual that causes a spirit to reside there. But whatever it is, something seems to have drawn a large number of spirits back to the site of the tragedy. And I believe it is the nature of the event that took a person's life.

There are many reasons to believe that the spirits who haunt these places do so because of the ways these people died. I believe that sometimes the spirits have a desire to make themselves known to call attention to an unsolved murder. They make themselves known by paranormal sightings, sounds, and smells. In other words: If a spirit is present, then at sometime in the history of the site, there has probably been a murder, and the one who did the murder was never prosecuted. Psychic Carol Pate noted that every spirit she encountered in El Dorado seemed to be in great distress. It seems that some tragic event troubles them. However, in other places, such as Colonial Williamsburg, there are stories of ghosts dancing. It may be that in other locals, spirits are present because they are returning to a happy place. But in El Dorado, tragic misdeeds and having spirits present seems a lot more than a coincidence.

Certainly, this is just a theory, but in downtown El Dorado there is a wealth of violent, recorded history that encompasses the downtown and the city blocks around the theater. Many of the stories that I have recorded are just that: undocumented stories. However, there seems to be more than a thread of truth woven through them.

Many of the tragic events of the 1920s oil boom are from oral histories recorded in the Arkansas Museum of Natural Resources. These numerous eyewitness accounts confirm the violent acts of murder, robbery, executions, and jilted lovers that are an interwoven part of this community's history. And if they have anything to do with the infestation of spirits, then the Rialto Theater and nearby blocks are very likely candidates to have a concentration of various spirit beings.

In addition, the desecration of the old slave cemetery and denying the mayhem and murders of the oil boom certainly proves another conclusion: The town has some secrets it has tried to hide. Of course, no community wants to be remembered for the sins of its past, but El Dorado seems to have an unnatural affinity for sweeping the gory, degrading, and lawless elements of its past neatly under the rug.

Finally, what do I believe, as one who has spent numerous hours documenting these unusual stories and events? After I considered all of the evidence that I uncovered, I have but one conclusion: The Rialto Theater and the city blocks surrounding the theater, are not only haunted by the ghosts or spirits of a few individuals, but the area is haunted by an untold number of spirits—possibly several hundred.

Many of them make themselves known by sounds, sights, and smells. And when you combine these paranormal occurrences with the thousands of energy imprints of tragedies noted by Ms. Pate, it seems clear to me, that these blocks in downtown El Dorado, Arkansas, are easily some of the most haunted locals in the United States.

But I have something else to add. Over the 35 years that I have lived in El Dorado, I have detected a pervasive negativism that infests the community. It seems to manifest itself in some individuals in an attitude of opposition to almost any civic or community improvement. I am convinced that the lawlessness of this town's early days, which carried over well into the late 1950s and '60s, made such a negative impact on the community that it distorted the vision of the generation who lived during this time.

However, during the last 10 years there has been surge of civic pride that has pushed the negative attitude out of the forefront of community talk. This negativity is still a small part of our town, but it is steadily shrinking as the last generation dies off and younger civic leaders take their place.

Of course, when paranormal occurrences are reported, there will always be individuals who will try to discount them. However, as one who had to have a paranormal experience in the theater in order to believe the spirits are present, I can assure you that these ghosts do exist.

The newspaper story in the next chapter is about an attempt to debunk the ghosts of the Rialto. This attempt to disprove paranormal activities associated with the theater was conducted by an *El Dorado News-Times* reporter and his friend.

31

A NIGHT IN THE THEATER

[Story by Brad McLelland for the *El Dorado News-Times Sunday News*]

Excerpts: On the night my friend and I were locked inside, Ada, who has owned the business for six years, took us on a tour of the building around 9 p. m., shortly before she closed the doors and left us to the silence. "I wish you luck" were her last words before leaving. For 72 years, no one has ever spent an entire night alone in the Rialto Theater, and her words bore a particularly unsettling undertone that night. This is my story of what happened that night...

There's a building on Cedar Street that speaks night and day. At certain times, disembodied voices drift down the hallways and wander into lonely crawl spaces. Sometimes you can hear them from the lobby; other times, if the streets outside are quiet, you can sense them when you're walking to your car. They are the ghosts of the Rialto Theater. Unlike traditional ghosts, the kind you might envision roaming cobwebbed corridors or floating in silent graveyards, the voices of these spirits belong to entertainers—Clark Gable, Vivian Leigh, Denzel Washington, Julia Roberts. Throughout the decades, night after night, entertainers like these have breathed life into cardboard-thin celluloid, and their voices carry through the Rialto's timeworn halls and stairways like a bold commentary on the immortal nature of art. But what happens when the projector stops and the audience goes home? What whispers fill the sudden void when everything becomes still, when the living voices die away in darkness?

Inside the wall of the Rialto Theater, the real ghosts come out to play.

Rising three stories above 113 East Cedar Street, the Rialto is one of the most renowned structures in this region, as mysterious as it is magnificent. Much of that mystery stems from urban legends arisen from there over the years past—stories of apparitions, unusual noises, and uncanny whiffs of perfume in vacant rooms. Are these stories true? Do spirits actually walk the winding staircases of El Dorado's premier playhouse-turned-cinema?

Many employees of the theater claim they do.

Sometimes it's not enough to accept the stories as they come; sometimes morbid curiosity gets the upper hand. That's why a friend and I decided to seek the truth ourselves and take our chances with the unknown—and to spend an entire night alone in "Arkansas' Last Grand Theater."

This we did on October 11th. We did not make it to sunrise.

(The couple has just walked into the lobby of the Rialto. It is after the last movie finished and the theater is empty. The following story is verbatim from the reporter's printed story.)

"The Rialto at night is an alien place. In the main lobby, a peeling statuette of a Greek woman holding water vessels stands atop a black leather banquette—something I've seen a million times but never quite like I did on October 11. In various corners, cardboard "stand-ups" of Hollywood's stars loom from their perches in nearby shadows.

My friend and I set up "camp" in the snack parlor, the place we felt most comfortable before setting out to explore. Armed with flashlights, a 35-millimeter camera, a video camera, a micro-cassette recorder, and snacks to last through the night, we embarked on our lonely journey into the main auditorium, the place where most "activity" has been witnessed over the years. Our plan was two-fold; Record any activity we might see, and watch the sunrise from the building's rooftop.

Strange sounds abounded throughout the night: creaks, rattles, groans, drips. As we took note of each, we were careful to distinguish the ordinary settling sounds an old building makes with more peculiar noises; we talked them out, tried to guess their origin . . . and tried to keep our cool. It's one thing to talk about doing what we were doing; it's another thing entirely to do it.

Our first objective was to get a photo of me sitting on the stage, behind the proscenium opening, with the curtain partially raised. El Dorado had gotten a good rain that day, and the vaulted ceiling trickled in places, causing light echoes in the cavernous auditorium.

It was sometime after 1 a.m. While we were shooting pictures, something caught my eye at the back of the room; a flicker in the projection booth. I motioned to my friend and began making my way off stage. My heart thudded heavily, but I told myself it was my imagination, only imagination. A moment later, my friend also noticed something and called my name urgently: another flicker—a shadow in the shape of a human torso, moving behind the parted curtains near the booth.

A feeling overtook me then that I can't fully describe: a mix of breathlessness and nausea, I guess. We directed our cameras to the areas in question, but caught nothing tangible. The air in the auditorium felt cold and clammy; I felt like a child who's just been goosed in the dark.

After scurrying back to base camp, we decided to "re-evaluate" what we'd seen, and made up our minds that our experience may have been psychosomatic: a blend of optical illusion and pure, old-fashioned panic. Resolved, we headed upstairs to explore the projection booth where employees were said to have smelled Penelope's perfume.

We'd taken note of many frightful-looking areas during our tour with Ada, one of those being the ancient rear basement which houses the dilapidated dressing rooms beneath the main stage. Another area hidden to the eye is a dusty, unused staircase used during the segregation days. The stairs are located behind a wall in the left portion of the balcony area; one must use caution exploring these stairs, and exercise a tremendous amount of bravery.

We videotaped our journey up and down the stairwell and made our way into the projection booth upstairs. For a while, we entertained ourselves with small tasks: exploring the attic, etching our names into a wall. Eventually, we noticed something odd: A door leading into the booth that had previously been open was now shut.

We scurried back downstairs.

Again, we decided on the psychosomatic argument; external factors—an interior breeze, maybe—had closed the door while we were downstairs. Nothing more.

Our argument did not hold up for long.

While we were huddled in the main lobby, we heard a series of noises that to this day we cannot explain. A loud crash from somewhere in the walls; a heavy creaking noise on the floor we'd just evacuated. We glanced at our watches. Only 2:45 a.m. A long way to go yet before the sunrise.

The final noise—the noise that sealed our decision to vacate the premises prematurely—came from the winding staircase to our left.

Not 10 feet from where we sat, came the unmistakable sound of footsteps. They creaked and crackled loudly— at least four times—on the paisley carpet, until at last they came to rest on the bottom step. We froze. Our hearts, which has already been beating out of control, banged like war drums.

A tear welled up in my friend's eye. I envisioned Penelope, dressed in flowing white garments, engulfed in a cloud of mist, stepping into the lobby.

Slowly, I shifted toward the cassette recorder, pressed record, and placed it on the banquette. Slinking back into the snack parlor, we collected our things.

Before we headed to the emergency door, we grabbed the recorder and asked ourselves, did we really want to leave? Did we really want to blow our opportunity to catch something concrete—an actual ghost—inside Arkansas' Last Grand Theater?

You bet we did. You might have too.

We left at 3 a.m. We did not look back.

Today, the contents of that recorded moment on Oct. 12 leave a strange, uncomfortable impression. But then again, there could be logical explanations for all of it, couldn't there?

Couldn't there?

I like to think of myself as a rational fellow, as sensible as I am open-minded. But every now and then, something comes along that casts a cold shadow on logic, and rationality tumbled under its weight. What dwells within the walls of the Rialto Theater that makes a grown man run and cower?

It's a fascinating question, and one I still hope to answer.

Someday I plan to return to the Rialto to finish my task, to etch my name into the wall again . . . and to see that sunrise.

***

Downtown El Dorado and the Rialto Theater await your visit.

The End, or is it just the beginning?